A Williamson  Little Hands® Book

# Animal Habitats!

Learning about North American animals & plants
through Art, Science & Creative Play

by Judy Press

Illustrated by Betsy Day

Williamson Books  Nashville, Tennessee

Library of Congress Cataloging-in-Publication Data

Press, Judy, 1944-
  Animal habitats! : learning about North American animals and plants through art,
science & creative play / by Judy Press ; illustrations by Betsy Day.
      p. cm. -- (A Williamson Little Hands book)
  Includes bibliographical references and index.
  ISBN 0-8249-6778-X (casebound : alk. paper) -- ISBN 0-8249-6756-9 (softcover : alk. paper)
  1. Habitat (Ecology)--Juvenile literature. 2. Habitat (Ecology)--Study and teaching--Activity programs. I. Day, Betsy, ill. II. Title. III. Series.
  QH541.14.P72 2005
  372.35'7--dc22
                                      2005014258

Little Hands® series editor: **Susan Williamson**
Project editor: **Lisa Trumbauer**
Interior design: **Nancy-jo Funaro**
Interior illustrations: **Betsy Day**
Cover design and illustration: **Michael Kline**

Published by Williamson Books
An imprint of Ideals Publications
A division of Guideposts
535 Metroplex Drive, Suite 250
Nashville, Tennessee 37211
800-586-2572


Printed and bound in Italy by Lego.
10 9 8 7 6 5 4 3 2 1

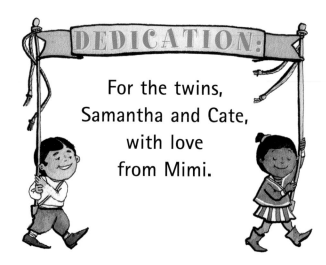

DEDICATION:

For the twins,
Samantha and Cate,
with love
from Mimi.

# CONTENTS

# CONTENTS

* Mostly easy
** A bit more difficult
*** Most challenging

# A Habitat Is a Home

## WHERE DO YOU LIVE?

The places where we live are called our communities. My community is the city of Pittsburgh in the state of Pennsylvania. I live in a red brick house, and my back yard has trees and a small stream. When I look out my kitchen window, I see birds and squirrels and chipmunks.

When I'm hungry, I go to the grocery store to buy food. When I'm cold, I turn on the heat, and when I'm warm, I turn on the air-conditioning. If I want a drink of water, I turn on the faucet.

My community is the place where I find everything I need to live and grow. It has air to breathe and shelter to keep me safe from the weather. My community also has people and friends and shops—and plants and animals, too.

## WHERE DO PLANTS AND ANIMALS LIVE?

Animals and plants also live in communities. Their community is called a habitat. A habitat has everything the plants and animals need. A habitat has food, water, shelter, and air that plants and animals need to live and grow.

Not all plants and animals need the same things. For example, a frog eats different foods than a bear. A salmon in a river has different needs than a lizard in the desert. That is why our planet has different habitats— for the many different plants and animals that live here.

Some habitats are very large, like the Arctic tundra near the North Pole. Other habitats are small, like a pond. A fallen log can be a habitat, a park in a city can be a habitat, even your back yard is a habitat! Wherever plants and animals live naturally is a habitat. No matter how big or how small, each place is perfect for the plants and animals that live there. Let's explore some of the habitats of North America.

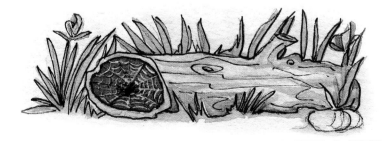

You are about to discover some of the plants and animals in eight different North American habitats. The pictures on these pages show each habitat. Look at each picture, and think about which each habitat might be like. What might a plant or animal need to live here?

What do you think a forest habitat is like?

What do you think the Arctic tundra habitat is like?

What do you think a desert habitat is like?

North American Habitats

What do you think a grasslands habitat is like?

What do you think river and lake habitats are like?

What do you think a wetlands habitat is like?

What do you think a seashore habitat is like?

What do you think a city habitat is like?

As you explore each habitat in this book, a ranger will tell you about it. You'll then discover the plants and animals on your own as you search the pictures and create the crafts.

So get out your crayons, markers, glue, paper, scissors, and other art stuff! It's time to meet the animals and plants that call each habitat home.

# Welcome to the Desert!

Do you remember ever being really, really thirsty? What was the weather like that day? Was it hot and sunny outside? And what did you do on such a hot, sunny day? Did you play quietly in the shade? Did you stay in an air-conditioned place? Or maybe you went swimming? Staying in cool places or swimming—that's how a lot of people stay cool on a hot day. On hot days, with very little rain, people and animals also need to drink a lot of water and stay cool. Plants need water, too.

A desert is a place that is very, very dry. It gets very little rain, or precipitation. Some deserts are hot. Some deserts are cold. Some deserts have sand and no plants. Other deserts are lush with cactuses and other plant life.

## What do all deserts have in common?

All deserts are dry places.

All deserts get very little precipitation.

Plants and animals that live in deserts learn to adapt to this dry climate. Even the hottest, driest desert can support an amazing variety of wildlife. In this chapter, we'll explore some of the plants and animals that live in the deserts of North America.

Look at this drawing of the desert.
Some of the projects in this chapter are
about these desert plants and animals.

Which plant has spiky
needles instead of leaves?

Which animal is a lizard?

Which animal is a bird?

Which animal is an insect?

# The Sonora Desert

The Sonora Desert gets more rain than any other desert in North America. The desert also has extreme temperature changes. Temperatures during the day can reach 120 degrees F (65 degrees C), and at night the temperature can drop down to freezing. If you lived here, you'd want to go swimming during the day, but you might wear a winter coat at night!

THE SONORA DESERT STRETCHES OVER PARTS OF SOUTHERN CALIFORNIA, ARIZONA, AND NORTHWESTERN MEXICO.

## TORN-PAPER SAGUARO CACTUS

Branches of the Colorado River run through the Sonora desert, so many trees, large cacti, and shrubs find enough water to grow here.

**WHAT YOU NEED:**

- Green and white construction paper
- Child safety scissors
- Glue stick
- Markers

**WHAT YOU DO:**

**1.** Tear or cut the green construction paper into the shape of the cactus. By tearing the paper, you get a more natural rough edge.

**2.** Cut out a window in the center of the cactus.

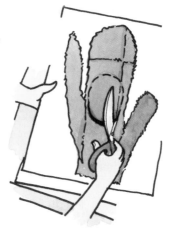

**3.** Glue the cactus to white paper.

**4.** Draw an owl inside the window on the white background paper.

**5.** Use a marker to draw the ridges and needles of the cactus.

## FIELD NOTES

Some desert animals use the saguaro cactus as a home. The Gila woodpecker, for example, creates nest holes in older saguaro stems. When nesting time is over, the woodpeckers move out. The holes are empty. Other animals, like insects, lizards, or pygmy owls, then move in! Who might live in the hole in your cactus? Cut additional holes in your torn-paper cactus, and draw other desert animals that might live there.

## Art Lesson

• Make a torn-paper collage of a desert scene. Tear different shapes from colored construction paper that look like desert rocks and sand. Paste the shapes onto paper. The rough edges make a unique design.

## DESERT SCIENCE

Many desert plants have *spines*, which are like sharp prickles, instead of leaves. The moisture stored in leaves can be more easily evaporated—soaked up—by the sun. But spines allow less evaporation, so less moisture escapes into the air.

# BUBBLE-PRINT GILA MONSTER

The Gila monster is a poisonous lizard named for the Gila River Basin of the southwestern United States. Are you named for a special person or place?

**WHAT YOU NEED:**

- Plastic bubble wrap
- Black and brown tempera paint
- Paintbrush
- White paper
- Child safety scissors
- Black marker
- Glue stick

**WHAT YOU DO:**

**1.** Lightly brush black and brown paint onto the bubble wrap.

**2.** While the paint is still wet, lay the white paper on top of the bubble wrap. Lightly press down then lift up for a print.

This is what a real Gila monster looks like.

**3.** Allow the paint to dry. Use a marker to draw a large Gila monster on your bubble print.

**4.** Cut out the Gila monster and glue it onto a different sheet of paper.

## WHAT'S IN A NAME?

Another reptile in the Sonora Desert is a sidewinder snake. Say the name again—sidewinder. Think about how this snake might move. Do you think it moves forward in a straight line? Or does it move sideways? Why do you think it moves sideways?

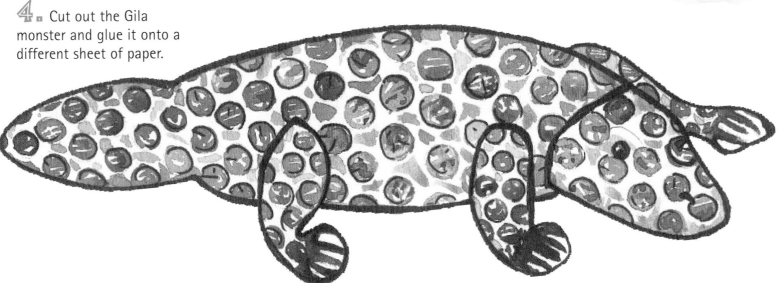

## FIELD NOTES

A Gila monster is a lizard, which is a type of reptile. Reptiles are cold-blooded. That means that their body temperature changes as the temperature outside changes. (Your body temperature always stays the same.) So in the summer, when the desert is very hot, the Gila monster is mostly active only at night, when the temperature is cooler. Gila monsters like to eat small mammals, birds, and eggs. In winter, when food is scarce, the Gila monster's body relies on the fat stored in its short, thick tail.

## Art Lesson

• Make other bubble-prints using different colors of paint. Cut out the shapes of other animals that have "bumpy" skin, such as an alligator or a seastar.

• What do you think of when you hear the word "monster"? Draw a picture of your idea of a monster.

# The Mohave Desert...

The Mohave Desert is the smallest of the four North American deserts. It has high mountains and several large water basins that lie below sea level.

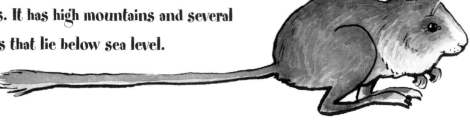

THE MOHAVE DESERT IS LOCATED IN SOUTHEASTERN CALIFORNIA, SOUTHERN NEVADA, EXTREME SOUTHWESTERN UTAH, AND NORTHWESTERN ARIZONA.

## PAPER-PLATE KANGAROO RAT

The desert kangaroo rat does not need to drink water to live! Its body has adapted to desert life so that it doesn't need liquids.

**WHAT YOU DO:**

**WHAT YOU NEED:**

- Small white paper plate
- Black marker
- Brown crayon
- Scrap of white paper
- Child safety scissors
- Transparent tape

**1.** Fold the paper plate in half. The rounded edge of the plate is the top of the kangaroo rat. The flat edge is the bottom of the kangaroo rat.

**2.** Draw the rat's eyes, nose, mouth, ears, and feet on both sides of the folded paper plate.

**3.** Color both sides of the plate brown. (Leave a small white stripe along the bottom edge.)

**4.** Cut out a tail from white paper. Color it brown. Tape the tail inside the plate.

**5.** Tape the edges of the plate together.

☛ **TRY THIS!** The desert kangaroo rat hops on its hind feet, and it uses its tail for balance. Try hopping on one foot. Count the number of times you can hop without losing your balance.

### Art Lesson

• You can make many animals using a folded paper plate. Add wings for a bird, a long neck for a swan, or make up your own animal.

### WHAT'S IN A NAME?

Now that you have "met" the kangaroo rat, think about another kangaroo you may have seen in pictures or at the zoo. Look at the picture of the kangaroo rat on page 14. Compare the kangaroo rat with the kangaroo shown here. What do the two animals have in common? How are the two animals different? How do you think the kangaroo rat got its name?

# ROLLING ROADRUNNER

Roadrunners can fly, but they are much better runners. They can scoot along the ground at about 15 miles (24 kilometers) per hour. That's about five times faster than a grown-up person can walk!

**WHAT YOU NEED:**

- White construction paper
- Black marker
- Child safety scissors
- Glue
- Crayons
- Pencil
- Paper fastener

**WHAT YOU DO:**

**1.** Place your hand on white paper, and close your fingers. (Do not spread them open.) Trace your hand, and cut it out. This will be the birds tail feathers.

**2.** Draw an oval on another piece of white paper. This will be the bird's body. Then draw the bird's head. Cut the body and the head out, too.

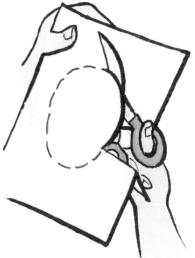

**3.** Glue the handprint tail feathers on one end of the oval. Glue the head to the other end of the oval.

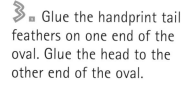

**4.** Draw and color your roadrunner.

**5.** What is your roadrunner missing? It's missing its legs and feet! Draw a circle on the white paper, and cut it out.

**6.** Draw three bird's legs and feet around the paper circle.

**7.** Attach the circle to the bird, using a paper fastener.

## FIELD NOTES

Roadrunners build their nests from small sticks. The female (mother) bird builds the shallow, saucer-like nest in a low bush, cactus, or small tree. Have you ever seen a bird's nest? What did it look like? How was it the same or different from the roadrunner's nest?

**8.** Turn the circle to make your roadrunner run!

☞ **TRY THIS!** Roadrunners are so quick that they're one of the few animals that can catch rattlesnakes! Using their wings like a cape, they snap up the rattlesnake by the snake's tail. How fast can you run? Have a friend use a second hand to see. If you don't have a second hand, count out the seconds slowly, like this: "One roadrunner, two roadrunners, three roadrunners." Keep going!

# The Chihuahua Desert

The Chihuahua Desert is the largest desert in North America. Like all deserts, it is very dry. It gets less than 10 inches of rain a year. Most of the rain falls during the summer.

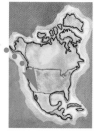

MOST OF THE CHIHUAHUA DESERT LIES SOUTH OF THE BORDER BETWEEN THE UNITED STATES AND MEXICO. IN THE UNITED STATES, THIS DESERT EXTENDS INTO PARTS OF NEW MEXICO, TEXAS, AND SOUTHEASTERN ARIZONA.

## EGG-CARTON RATTLESNAKE

**WHAT YOU NEED:**

- Styrofoam egg carton
- Child safety scissors
- 2 pipe cleaners
- Red paper
- Glue

**WHAT YOU DO:**

**1.** Cut apart the twelve cups of the egg carton.

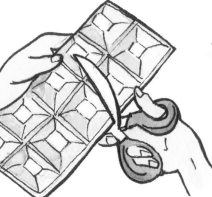

**2.** Twist together two pipe cleaners to make one long pipe cleaner.

**3.** Thread the pipe cleaner through the center of each egg-carton cup. Make sure the cups are all facing the same direction.

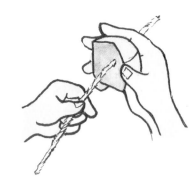

**4.** Twist one end of the pipe cleaner to form the snake's rattle.

**5.** Cut out a forked tongue from red paper. Glue the tongue to the front of the snake.

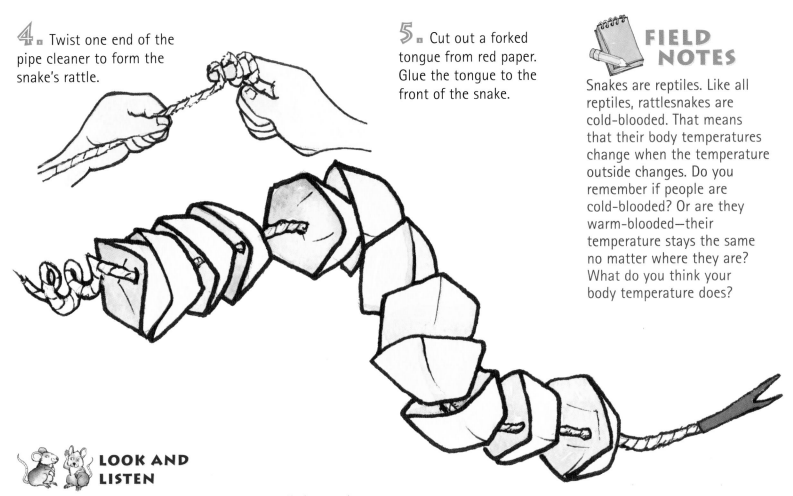

## FIELD NOTES

Snakes are reptiles. Like all reptiles, rattlesnakes are cold-blooded. That means that their body temperatures change when the temperature outside changes. Do you remember if people are cold-blooded? Or are they warm-blooded—their temperature stays the same no matter where they are? What do you think your body temperature does?

## LOOK AND LISTEN

The rattlesnake has a hollow rattle on its tail that makes a buzzing sound when it moves. Shake your egg carton rattlesnake. What sound does it make? Do you think that the sound of a rattlesnake's rattle helps the snake? Or does the sound help its prey—animals the rattlesnake wants to eat? Why might a rattlesnake shake its rattle?

☞ **TRY THIS!** Ask a grown-up to take your temperature on a day when it is warm outside, and then on a day when it is cold outside. Did your temperature change with the outdoor temperature, or did it stay the same? If your temperature stayed the same, you are not cold-blooded, like a snake. Like all humans, you are warm-blooded.

# HAIRPIN STINK BEETLE

Stink beetles get their names because of their stinky smell. If you go to a desert, you'll probably see a stink beetle. They are one of the most common insects in the desert.

## WHAT YOU NEED:

- 3 hairpins
- Popsicle stick
- Glue
- Black construction paper
- Pencil
- Child safety scissors

## WHAT YOU DO:

**1.** Pull apart the hairpins so they form right angles, like the corner of a square. These are the beetle's legs.

**2.** Glue the hairpin legs to the Popsicle stick.

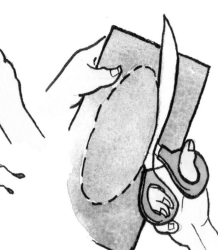

**3.** On black paper, draw and cut out the following shapes: a thin oval; a circle; a second circle slightly smaller; and two very thin rectangles for antennae.

**4.** Cut a slit in the center of the oval for the wings. Glue the wings onto the Popsicle stick, over the hairpins.

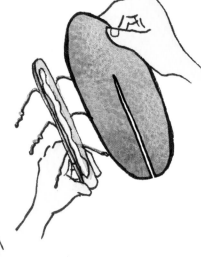

**5.** Glue the circles and the antennae to the stick, again over the hairpins.

## FIELD NOTES

When frightened, stink beetles stand on their front hands, like a handstand! They bend their front legs down, and they lift their rear legs into the air. The beetle makes this pose to defend itself. In this position, the beetle looks bigger and more scary. Also, with its rear end up in the air, its stink is more obvious! What body poses do people make so they look bigger or more scary?

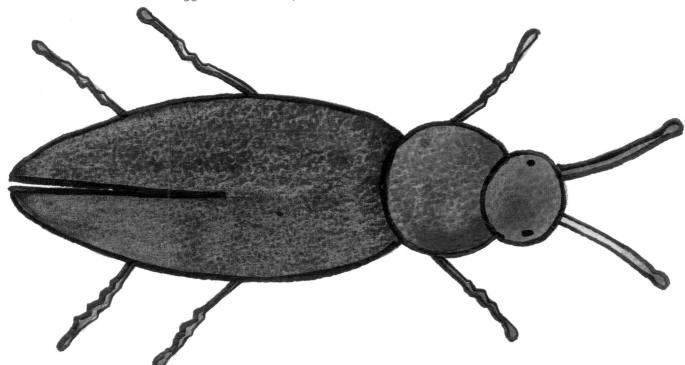

**Little Hands Story Corner™**

Read *Deserts* by Seymour Simon.

☛ **TRY THIS!** Stink beetles are great walkers. They stroll around the desert, looking for food. Make two hairpin stink beetles. Tie a string around the front of each Popsicle stick. Then give one hairpin stink beetle to a friend. Place the beetles at the end of a table, and pull the strings. Have a race to see which one goes the fastest.

# The Great Basin Desert

The Great Basin is not the largest desert in North America, but it is the largest desert in the United States. It is a "cool" or cold desert, and it snows here in the winter. Temperatures are not very high because this desert is farther north than other deserts. Also, the land sits at a higher level—air is cooler higher up.

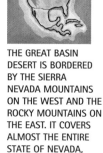

THE GREAT BASIN DESERT IS BORDERED BY THE SIERRA NEVADA MOUNTAINS ON THE WEST AND THE ROCKY MOUNTAINS ON THE EAST. IT COVERS ALMOST THE ENTIRE STATE OF NEVADA, AS WELL AS PARTS OF UTAH, CALIFORNIA, AND IDAHO.

## FINGERPRINT PICKLEWEED

Pickleweed is a plant. It provides food for birds and mammals of the Great Basin Desert. Its leaves look like little pickles strung on thin wires.

**WHAT YOU NEED:**

- Green tempera paint
- Shallow dish or lid
- Construction paper (any light color)
- Rag (to wipe off your fingers)

**WHAT YOU DO:**

1. Pour a thin layer of paint into the dish or lid.

2. Dip your finger into the paint.

3. Press your finger onto the paper.

4. Continue dipping and pressing to make the shape of the pickleweed. Look at the picture on the next page to see what a pickleweed really looks like.

## FIELD NOTES

The land of the Great Basin Desert is very salty. Pickleweed plants have learned how to adapt to this salty environment. When pickleweed roots soak up moisture from the ground, they also absorb salt. The plant stores the salt in its tips. When the tips become full of salt, they turn red. Then they fall off. Do you think the tip of a pickleweed tastes sweet or salty? What about the rest of the pickleweed plant?

☞ **TRY THIS!** Count the fingerprint "pickles" on your pickleweed picture. How many pickleweeds are on each branch? If you make your pickleweed bigger, how many "pickles" can you add?

### Art Lesson

• Make several fingerprints on paper. Use a pen to draw animals or people from each print.

# PAPER-PLATE BIGHORN SHEEP

Bighorn sheep get their name from—can you guess? Right! These sheep have big horns on their heads. Bighorn sheep, or mountain sheep, like to live in large groups, called herds. A male (boy) sheep with big horns is usually the leader of the herd. Females (girls) also have horns, but their horns are shorter than the males' horns. Look at this picture. Which bighorn sheep is the female? Which is the male?

**WHAT YOU NEED:**

- Large white paper plate
- Child safety scissors
- Brown crayon
- Black marker
- Transparent tape
- Cardboard toilet-paper tube

**WHAT YOU DO:**

**1.** Cut off the rim of the paper plate. You should have one long piece.

**2.** Cut the rim in half. Cut around the end of each rim for horns.

**3.** Cut out the sheep's head and ear from the center of the paper plate.

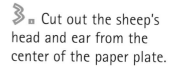

**4.** Color the face brown. Use a marker to draw the sheep's eyes and muzzle. The muzzle is the nose area.

**5.** Tape the horns and ear to the sheep's head.

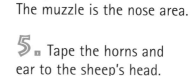

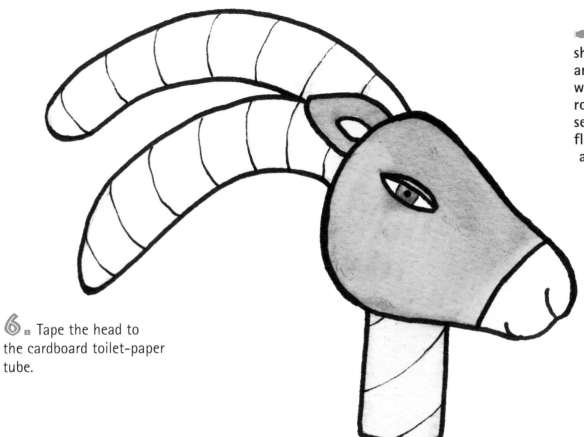

**6.** Tape the head to the cardboard toilet-paper tube.

☞ **TRY THIS!** Bighorn sheep are sure-footed animals. Their feet move well on mountains and rocky cliffs. Scatter several pillows on the floor. Pretend the pillows are the uneven ground of a rocky desert. Take off your shoes, and walk from pillow to pillow. Do your feet slip, or do they grip?

 ## LOOK AND LISTEN

Male bighorn sheep often compete to see who is better. They rush at each other and bang horns. What do you think the sound of the crashing horns sounds like? Try to bang two objects together to make such a sound, like two books or two wooden blocks.

## WHAT'S IN A NAME?

The pocket mouse is small enough to fit in your—yes!—pocket. The pocket mouse and the bighorn sheep both live in the Great Basin Desert and both have descriptive names. What's the describing word in the sheep's name? In the mouse's name? What do these names tell you about each animal?

# Welcome to the Forest!

Have you ever taken a walk in the woods with your family? Or have you ever read or heard stories that take place in the woods, like "Goldilocks and the Three Bears" or "Little Red Riding Hood"? The settings for these stories, and the places where you've walked with your family, are forests. A forest is a natural habitat—a community where plants and animals all live together.

Some forests have trees with leaves that change color in the fall. Some forests have trees that stay green all year long. Some forests have trees that are so big you can't wrap your arms around them. And some forests are so rainy and warm that many different plants and animals live there.

## What do all forests have in common?

All forests have trees.

All forests get enough rain for trees to grow.

The trees provide not only homes (or shelter) for the animals, but the trees provide food for the animals, too. In this chapter, we'll discover specific trees and animals that live in the various forests of North America—the deciduous forest, the coniferous forest, the temperate rain forest, and the tropical rain forest.

Some forest animals might be familiar to you. See if you recognize these forest animals. You'll learn more about them with the projects in this chapter.

Which animal has antlers on its head?

Which animal looks like it is wearing a mask?

Which animals fly? (One is hanging upside down!)

# Deciduous Forest

A deciduous (duh-SI-jue-us) forest has trees that change with the season. In the fall, some trees have leaves that turn brilliant shades of red, yellow, and orange. Eventually the leaves turn brown and fall to the ground. During the winter, the trees are bare, and in spring, new leaves begin to grow.

## AUTUMN LEAF RUBBINGS

**WHAT YOU NEED:**

- Leaves
- Thin white paper
- Crayons (fall colors)
- Child safety scissors
- Construction paper
- Glue stick

**WHAT YOU DO:**

**1.** First you need to find some leaves. Go outdoors with an older family member or a friend to look for leaves. The best leaves are ones that have a simple shape. Also feel the "back" of the leaf. The lines you feel are the leaf's veins. Leaves with distinct veins are good for tracing.

**2.** Back inside, place a leaf under the thin white paper, with the vein side facing up.

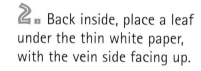

**3.** Rub a crayon over the white paper. Try to choose a color that matches the fall color of your leaf. As you rub, the image of the leaf will appear on the paper.

**4.** Repeat Step 3 for other leaves you've found.

**5.** Cut out your leaf rubbings.

**6.** Glue them to construction paper.

## FIELD NOTES

Forests are full of trees. Another word for a forest is a woodland. The trees provide shelter and food for animals. Many animals live in the trees or build their homes there. Animals might also eat the leaves or the nuts that fall from the tree. Think about the ways that you use trees. How do you use a tree on a hot, sunny day? How do you use a tree to have fun? How might people use the wood from a tree?

☞ **TRY THIS!** Leaves of deciduous trees come in many shapes and sizes. Each shape and size tells what tree the leaf belonged to. Go on a nature walk with a grown-up. Gather some leaves that have fallen off trees. Then go to the library and get a nature guide about trees that grow in your area. Try to match the leaves you found with the trees in the book. Which trees grow in your area?

### Art Lesson

• Make rubbings of other objects you find outdoors, such as: the bark of a tree trunk, a rough concrete sidewalk, the side of a building, a smooth stone.

# PAPER-CHAIN WOOLLY BEAR CATERPILLAR

Did you know that caterpillars are actually young butterflies or moths? It's true! A caterpillar will one day change into a butterfly or a moth through a process called metamorphosis. The woolly bear caterpillar will one day be a moth. Moths are active at night, unlike butterflies, which are active during the day. When are you most active?

## WHAT YOU NEED:

- Black and orange construction paper
- Child safety scissors
- Ruler (optional)
- Transparent tape
- Marker
- Wiggly eyes (optional)*

## WHAT YOU DO:

**1.** Cut out four strips from orange construction paper, and three strips from black construction paper. The strips should be about 1-1/2" x 6" (3.75 cm x 15 cm).

**2.** Tape the ends of each strip together so each strip forms a circle.

**3.** Tape the circles together so the colors resemble the colors of the woolly bear caterpillar: orange, black, orange, orange, orange, black, black.

**4.** Draw eyes and a mouth on the first orange circle. If you have wiggly eyes, glue them on instead of drawing them.

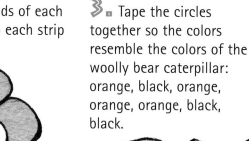

*Warning! Small beads pose a choking danger to young children. Grown-ups should control the supply and insert them into the project.

## FIELD NOTES

The woolly bear caterpillar hibernates in winter under tree bark, a rock, or a fallen log. (When an animal hibernates, it goes into a deep, sleeplike state for many weeks or months.) When the caterpillar wakes up, it is spring. The caterpillar eats leaves and weeds, then it begins to form a cocoon. After about two weeks, a beautiful Isabella tiger moth comes out of the cocoon. Why do you think you mostly see moths on warm, summer nights and not in the winter?

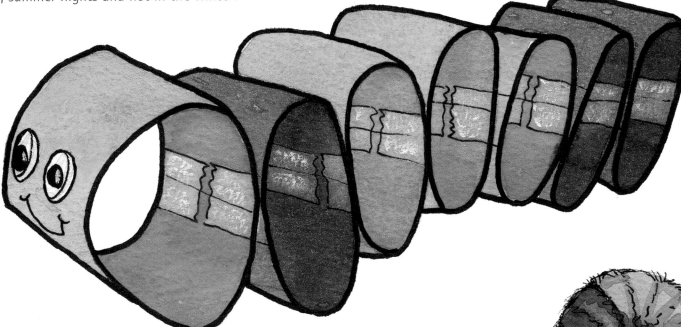

## WHAT'S IN A NAME?

Another name for the woolly bear caterpillar is the hedgehog caterpillar. The hedgehog is an animal that curls into a tight bristly ball and "plays dead" to protect itself. Look at this picture of the wooly bear caterpillar protecting itself. Why is *hedgehog caterpillar* a good name for it?

# PAPER-PLATE RACCOON MASK

If you walked through a forest during the day, you probably wouldn't see a raccoon. Raccoons are nocturnal—they are active mostly at night. They have a bushy, striped tail and black patches around their eyes. The patches make the raccoon look like it is wearing a mask. Raccoons are great tree climbers, but they can also swim and run across the ground. What different activities can you do? Can you climb trees, swim, and run?

## WHAT YOU NEED:

- Large white paper plate
- Child safety scissors
- Black crayon
- Regular scissors (ask a grown-up to help)
- Black pom-pom
- Glue
- Hole punch
- Ribbon or yarn

## WHAT YOU DO:

**1.** Draw a curved line across the center of the paper plate, like the line shown here.

**2.** Cut the plate on the curved line. Use the top half for your mask.

**3.** Draw the features of the raccoon's face on the plate. Draw circles for eyes, color black patches around the eyes, and draw whiskers.

**4.** Ask a grown-up to help cut out eye holes with regular scissors.

**5.** Glue on a pom-pom for the raccoon's nose.

**6.** From the leftover paper plate, cut out half-ovals for ears.

**7.** Glue the ears to the top of the mask.

**8.** Punch a hole on each side of the mask, toward the bottom.

**9.** Thread yarn through each hole, and tie a knot so the yarn is secure.

**10.** Place the mask against your face. Ask a grown-up to tie the ends of the yarn together to hold your mask in place.

## FIELD NOTES

Raccoons use their paws for more than just climbing or walking. Each paw has separate "digits," or fingers. Raccoons hold their food with their fingers when eating, just like people do. In fact, the Native Americans called the raccoon "arakum," which means "he scratches with hands." Today, we say the word "arakum" as *raccoon*. Why is this Native American word a good one to describe a raccoon?

## Art Lesson

• Use paper plates to make different animal masks. Cut out tall, pointed ears for a rabbit; short ears for a dog; or even antlers for a deer. What other animal masks could you make?

**Little Hands Story Corner™**

Read *Raccoon on His Own* by Jim Arnosky.

# EGG-CARTON EASTERN RED BAT

Forests are perfect habitats for the Eastern red bat because Eastern red bats like to live, or roost, within the thick leaves of a tree. During the day, the bat will hang from a branch from one leg, looking like a tree leaf. Why do you think it is helpful to the bat to look like a leaf?

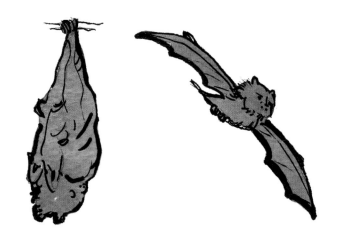

## WHAT YOU NEED:

- Cardboard egg carton
- Child safety scissors
- Red tempera paint
- Paintbrush
- Red construction paper
- Pencil
- White craft glue
- Black marker
- String or yarn

## WHAT YOU DO:

**1.** Cut out one cup from a cardboard egg carton. Trim around the edges of the cup so the cup lays flat.

**2.** Paint the egg-carton cup red.

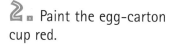

RED

**3.** On red construction paper, draw the shape of a bat's wings. Cut it out.

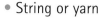

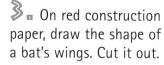

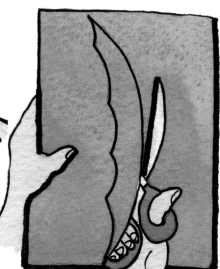

**4.** Glue the edges of the egg-carton cup to the center of the red construction-paper wings.

**5.** Draw the bat's eyes, nose, and mouth on the egg-carton cup.

**6.** Poke a hole in the side of the egg-carton cup, above the bat's face.

## FIELD NOTES

Like many bats, the Eastern red bat eats insects. When the sun sets, the bat leaves its roost and begins flying around, looking for tasty insects, like mosquitoes, to eat. Bats eat so many insects that they help control the insect population. Imagine if the world did not have bats. What would the nighttime be like if more mosquitoes buzzed around?

**7.** Thread string through the hole and tie it securely.

**8.** Dangle the bat by the string to make it fly.

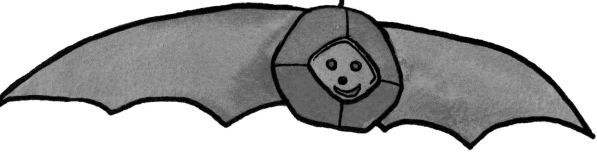

## LOOK AND LISTEN

Bats find insects to eat mostly by their sense of hearing. They use a system called echolocation. The bat makes a very high-pitched sound that travels through the air. (Humans can't hear it.) The sound bounces off an insect, or echoes, back to the bat. The bat then pinpoints the insect's location by the echo. See if you can locate someone by a sound. Close your eyes, and follow the sound of someone's voice until you stand in front of him or her. Did you find the task easy or hard? Why might echolocation be a good listening system for bats flying around at night?

# Coniferous Forest

Most trees in a coniferous forest are evergreens. Evergreens don't lose their leaves in the fall, so evergreens stay green all year. The evergreen's leaves are shaped like needles. Compare a broad leaf from a deciduous tree with a needle leaf from an evergreen. How are the leaves different?

## PAPER-TRIANGLE PINE TREES

**WHAT YOU NEED:**

- Green and black construction paper
- Child safety scissors
- Glue
- Dark marker
- White tempera paint, in a dish or lid
- Clean kitchen sponge

**WHAT YOU DO:**

**1.** Cut out triangles from green construction paper. The triangles can be different sizes. The triangles will be the trees.

**2.** Glue the triangle trees to black paper.

**3.** Use dark marker to draw in details.

**4.** Dip a sponge into white paint. Press the sponge to the trees to make snow.

## FOREST SCIENCE

The needles of a coniferous tree have a thick, waxy skin. This helps the tree survive the winter because the needles don't lose a lot of water. Try it! Get a crayon (crayons are made out of wax) and two sheets of paper. Rub a crayon over one sheet. Then spill a few drops of water on both sheets. Which sheet soaks up the water? On which sheet does the water roll off? The water doesn't soak through the wax. The water inside an evergreen needle doesn't soak through the needle's wax, so more water stays inside.

## FIELD NOTES

Coniferous forests are also called boreal or taiga forests. Winters in a coniferous forest are usually very cold, and the season for growing new plants is usually short. The seeds of coniferous trees are found in cones, sometimes called pinecones. Some people use pinecones for decorations. What could you do with a pinecone?

# CEREAL-BOX MOOSE MASK

Moose are the largest members of the deer family. Animals in this family have hooves, long legs, and long bodies. Most male deer grow antlers, too, including the moose. The antlers of the male moose are usually bigger than the antlers of the female moose. Look at the moose in this picture. Do you think it is a male or a female? How can you tell?

## WHAT YOU NEED:

- Cardboard from a cereal box
- Pencil
- Child safety scissors
- Regular scissors (ask a grown-up for help!)
- Brown crayon
- Brown construction paper
- White glue

## WHAT YOU DO:

**1.** Cut off one big side from a box of cereal.

**2.** On the gray side, draw a simple outline of a moose's head, like the one shown here.

**3.** Cut out the moose's head from the cardboard. Ask a grown-up to help cut out eyeholes with regular scissors.

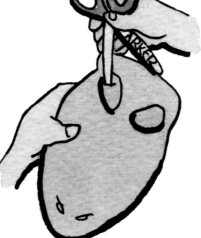

**4.** Color the moose's head brown.

**5.** Trace two hands on brown paper, and cut them out. These are the moose's antlers.

**6.** Also from the brown paper, cut out the moose's ears and dewlap or bell—the part that hangs down from the moose's chin.

**7.** Now put it all together! Glue on the antlers, the ears, and the dewlap.

**8.** Cut off one thin side of your cereal box. Glue it to the back of the moose's head so it forms a handle.

**9.** Hold the mask up to your face by the handle.

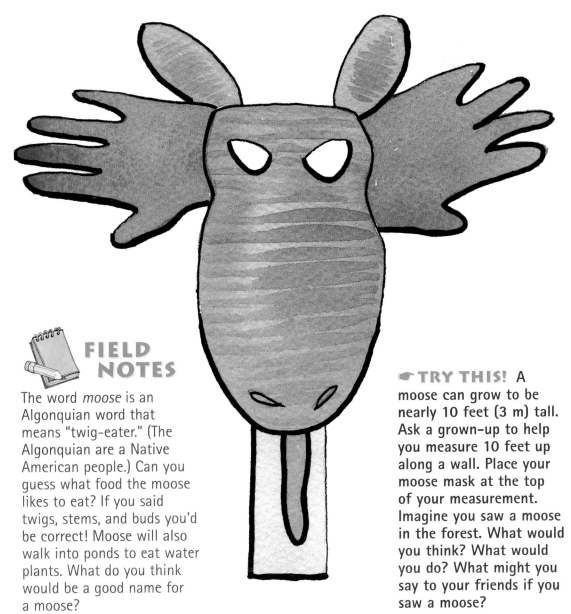

### FIELD NOTES

The word *moose* is an Algonquian word that means "twig-eater." (The Algonquian are a Native American people.) Can you guess what food the moose likes to eat? If you said twigs, stems, and buds you'd be correct! Moose will also walk into ponds to eat water plants. What do you think would be a good name for a moose?

☛**TRY THIS!** A moose can grow to be nearly 10 feet (3 m) tall. Ask a grown-up to help you measure 10 feet up along a wall. Place your moose mask at the top of your measurement. Imagine you saw a moose in the forest. What would you think? What would you do? What might you say to your friends if you saw a moose?

# BALD EAGLE FAN

A bald eagle is a bird of prey. That means that bald eagles hunt other animals for food. Bald eagles like to eat fish, so they usually live near the water, like a lake, a river, even an ocean. You can recognize a bald eagle by the white feathers on its head, which make it look "bald." How do you recognize other animals? What features make them special?

## WHAT YOU NEED:

- White construction paper
- Black marker
- Child safety scissors
- Brown and yellow crayons
- Brown construction-paper square, 8" x 8" (20 cm x 20 cm)
- Pencil
- Yarn or string

## WHAT YOU DO:

**1.** Draw the shape of a bald eagle's body, without the wings, on white construction paper. Use the image here to guide you. Cut out your drawing.

**2.** Draw black lines on the eagle's body for its tail feathers, the feathers around its neck, its eyes, and its beak. Draw on both sides of the cutout.

**3.** Color the beak yellow and the body brown. Don't color the tail feathers or the head. Leave them white. Again, color both sides of the cutout.

**4.** Accordion-fold the brown construction-paper square. This will be the bald eagle's wings.

**5.** Cut a slit in the center of the eagle.

**6.** Insert the wings through the slit.

**7.** Poke a hole in the top of the eagle with a pencil point.

**8.** Thread string through the hole and tie it to the eagle.

**9.** Dangle the string to make your eagle fly.

**☞ TRY THIS!** The bald eagle is the national bird of the United States. Look closely at a dollar bill. Can you find the bald eagle? Look for bald eagles on coins, stamps, flagpoles, even buildings.

### FIELD NOTES

Bald eagles build their nests in tall trees or on cliffs. The nest is made from twigs and leaves. It can measure up to 8 feet across and weigh as much as a ton! (One ton = 2,000 pounds.) Lay four bed pillows, end to end, on the floor. This is how big a bald eagle's nest may be. Now rest on the pillows and pretend you're a bald eagle.

### Little Hands Story Corner™

A baby eagle is called an eaglet. Read *Eaglet's World* by Evelyn White Minshull.

# Temperate Rain Forest

The trees in a temperate rain forest are mostly conifers, or evergreens. They are not only among the oldest trees in the world, but, like the giant sequoia, among the biggest. Can you wrap your arms around trees where you live? You can't wrap your arms around a giant sequoia! It's too big!

## FOLDED-PAPER GIANT SEQUOIA

### WHAT YOU NEED:

- Green construction paper
- Child safety scissors
- Transparent tape
- Green and brown crayons

### WHAT YOU DO:

**1.** Cut the green construction paper in half the long way.

**2.** Tape the two halves together, end to end, so you have one long strip.

**3.** Draw a giant tree trunk two-thirds of the way up the strip.

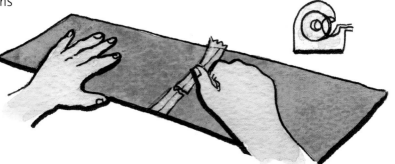

**4.** Draw branches and leaves on the top third of the strip.

**5.** Accordion-fold the strip.

**6.** Unfold the strip to watch your giant sequoia tree grow.

**FIELD NOTES**

The difference between deciduous and coniferous forests and a temperate rain forest is that the temperate rain forest gets much more rain. It can rain as much as 60 to 200 inches each year here. Temperate rain forests grow along the northwestern coast of North America. Other moisture comes from the fog that blows in from the ocean. How is this forest different from a desert? How is the weather different from the weather where you live?

☛ **TRY THIS!** The sequoia trees were around during the time of the dinosaurs. Draw a picture of a dinosaur surrounded by sequoia trees. How big should the dinosaur be compared to the sequoia tree? Here's a hint: A giant sequoia tree can grow as tall as 300 feet (90 m), while the Sauroposeidon dinosaur, the tallest of the dinosaurs, was about 60 feet (18 m) tall.

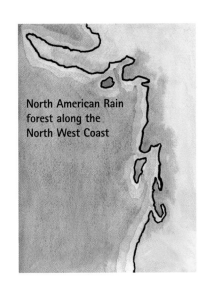

North American Rain forest along the North West Coast

# SLIDING BANANA SLUG

Banana slugs may be small, but they play an important role in the temperate rain forest. Banana slugs are decomposers. That means that the banana slug chews up leaves and other dead plant material that it finds as it crawls along the forest floor. In a way, you could say that the banana slug helps keep the forest floor clean. What do you think could happen if banana slugs did not live in the temperate rain forest?

## WHAT YOU NEED:

- White business-size envelope
- Markers or crayons
- Child safety scissors
- Yellow construction paper

## WHAT YOU DO:

**1.** Draw a forest scene on the front of a white envelope.

**2.** Cut out a window in the bottom of the envelope, but don't cut out the back of the envelope. This can be tricky, so ask a grown-up if you need help.

**3.** Cut out a long strip from yellow construction paper.

**4.** Draw a row of banana slugs across the yellow strip.

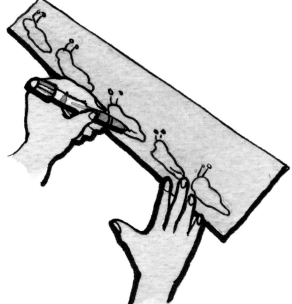

**5.** Cut a slit in each side of the envelope, wide enough for the strip of paper to slip through. This can also be tricky, so ask a grown-up if you need help.

**6.** Slowly pull the strip through the slits in the envelope. Your banana slug will move across the forest floor.

## FIELD NOTES

As the banana slug travels across the forest floor, it leaves behind a trail of slime. The slime keeps the slug's skin moist. The slime also helps the slug to breathe, and it makes it easier for the slug to crawl. Slime also keeps predators away because the predators don't like the slime. What would you do if you saw a banana slug?

### WHAT'S IN A NAME?

Why do you think this slug is called a banana slug? Look at the picture of the real banana slug on the previous page. What do you think?

# Tropical Rain Forest

Tropical rain forests are the rainiest habitats on the planet. They are lush and warm all year long. More kinds of animals and plants live in tropical rain forests than anywhere else on Earth. In North America, you find tropical rain forests in parts of Mexico.

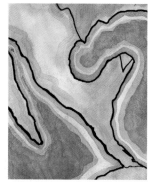

Rain Forest on the Yucatan Peninsula

## TROPICAL RAIN FOREST COLLAGE

**WHAT YOU NEED:**

- Old magazines
- Child safety scissors
- Green construction paper
- Glue stick
- Scraps of green paper (optional)

**WHAT YOU DO:**

1. Look through old magazines to find pictures of grass and trees. Rain forests are full of plantlife, so try to find as many pictures as possible. Cut them out.

2. Glue the pictures of the plants to a sheet of green construction paper. You can add scraps of green construction paper for an interesting look.

3. Now look through the magazines again, or other magazines. This time, look for tropical birds, insects, colorful frogs and butterflies, jaguars, and other animals that might live in a rain forest. You don't need as many animal pictures as plant pictures. Cut them out.

4. Glue the animal pictures to the plant pictures for a rain-forest collage. As you learn about other animals that live in the rain forest, draw pictures of them, cut them out, and add them to your collage.

A tropical rain forest has many layers. The top layer is called the emergent layer. This is where the tops of very tall trees poke through, or emerge from the top of the forest. The next layer is the canopy. This is where trees spread out their branches like a big umbrella. The next layer, the understory, is a layer of smaller trees and plants that grow below the canopy. The forest floor is the bottom layer.

Emergent layer →

Canopy →

Understory →

Forest floor →

## Art Lesson
• We get a lot of products from the rain forest, like bananas, coffee, tea, sugar, nuts, chocolate, cinnamon, papayas, and vanilla. Find pictures of some of these foods in magazines, cut them out, and add them to your tropical rain forest collage.

☛ **TRY THIS!** Think of the tropical rain forest as a house that has four floors or levels. The forest floor is the first floor; the understory is the second floor; the canopy is the third floor; and the emergent layer is the attic. Draw a picture of a forest, and surround the forest with the outline of a house. Divide the house into four levels. Go to the library, and research animals that live on each level. Draw the animals on the correct level of your rain-forest house.

# BROWN-BAG KINKAJOU

Kinkajous are part of the raccoon family. They live in trees, sleeping during the day, then coming out at night to look for food. They like to eat insects and fruit, and they use their long tongues to get to the fleshy part of a fruit or even the honey from a bee's nest. Think about what you learned about raccoons. How is the kinkajou like a raccoon?

**WHAT YOU NEED:**

- Small white paper plate
- Child safety scissors
- Black marker
- Brown crayon
- Glue stick
- Brown paper lunch bag

**WHAT YOU DO:**

**1.** Cut out the center of a small white paper plate. Do not throw away the rim.

**2.** Use a black marker to draw the kinkajou's face on the white paper-plate center. Color the face brown.

**3.** Cut out the kinkajou's tail and ears from the rim of the plate. Color them brown, too.

**4.** Glue the ears to the top of the kinkajou's head.

**5.** Glue the kinkajou's head to the bottom of the paper bag.

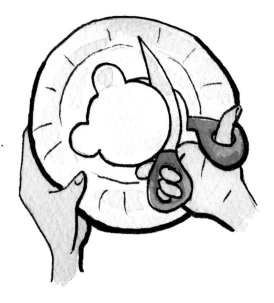

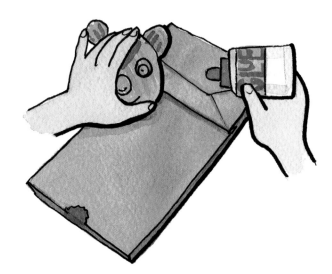

**6.** Glue the tail to the side of the bag, near the bottom.

**7.** Draw arms and paws on the front of the bag.

**8.** Slip your hand into the paper bag to use as a puppet.

## FIELD NOTES

Kinkajous travel along the treetops of the rain forest, holding on with their tails. The kinkajou's tail is called prehensile. That means that the tail is able to hold things by wrapping around them. What else might a kinkajou do as it travels across the treetops? Do you think it could swing from branch to branch with its tail?

☛ **TRY THIS!** Draw a picture of a kinkajou without its tail and cut it out. Cut out a curved tail from cardboard. (Cardboard will make a sturdier tail than paper.) Glue the tail to your kinkajou. Hook the tail over a pencil. Your kinkajou is using its tail to hold on! Hang your kinkajou from other objects around your home, perhaps even a houseplant.

# FOIL BLUE MORPHO BUTTERFLY

The blue morpho butterfly is one of the many insects that call the tropical rain forest home. The tops of their wings are a bright blue color, and the bottoms of their wings are a soft brown color. As the blue morphos flutter through the rain forest, they look like bright flashes of blue light.

### WHAT YOU NEED:

- Dark marker
- Yellow construction paper
- Child safety scissors
- Foil
- Blue plastic wrap
- Transparent tape
- Scrap of black construction paper
- Glue stick

### WHAT YOU DO:

**1.** Draw the outline of a butterfly's wings on yellow construction paper. Without cutting across the paper, cut out the butterfly wings and remove them.

**2.** Turn over the paper with the butterfly-shaped hole. Tape a sheet of blue plastic wrap over the butterfly-shaped hole.

**3.** Now tape a sheet of foil over the blue plastic wrap.

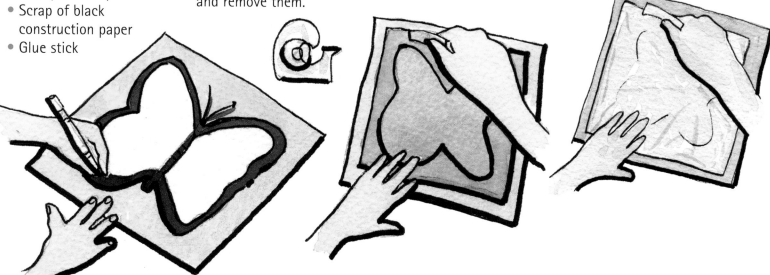

**4.** Turn the paper over. A blue, silvery color should come through the butterfly-shaped hole. Your butterfly's wings are a silvery blue, just like a blue morpho butterfly.

**5.** Draw and cut out the butterfly's body from black construction paper. Glue it to the center of the wings.

**6.** For the final touch, draw antennae on the butterfly's head.

## FIELD NOTES

When butterflies rest, they hold their wings closed above their bodies. Then the underside of the wings are exposed. Blue morphos often rest on the forest floor or within the understory. Why is soft brown a good color for the underside of a morpho butterfly's wings? How does the soft brown color help them?

☛ **TRY THIS!** Morpho butterflies taste with sensors that they have—on their legs! They smell the air with their antennas—which are a combination of tongues and noses! What part of your body helps you to taste? Place a peeled banana in front of you, then close your eyes. Touch it with a finger. Do you taste it? Now take a bite of the banana. What body part helps you to taste it?

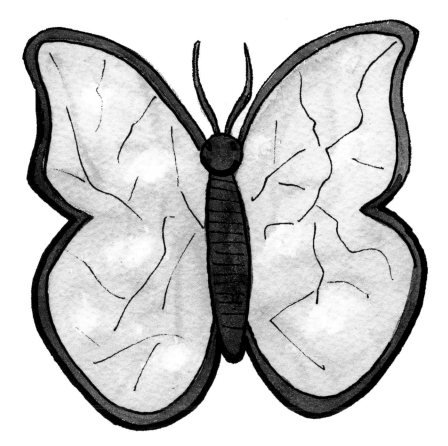

# Welcome to Rivers and Lakes!

Let's follow a river! A river begins high on top of a hill or a mountain. Water from rain and melting snow trickles down the mountain to form streams. These streams flow into one another, and together they become a fast-moving river. Where the land becomes flat, the river moves more slowly. The river becomes bigger and wider as it winds its way across the land. Eventually the river reaches the ocean, and the river water becomes part of the sea.

Now, let's pretend you dig a hole in your backyard. If you fill that hole with water, you will have made a very small lake. Lakes form when holes in the land fill with water from rivers, streams, or glaciers that melted long ago. Some lakes have rivers flowing into them, and some lakes have rivers flowing out of them.

## How are rivers and lakes different?

Rivers are ribbons of moving water.

Lakes are large pools of water surrounded by land.

Rivers and lakes make perfect habitats for both plants and animals. In this chapter, we'll explore these habitats as we learn about a few animals that make rivers and lakes their home.

# Who lives in rivers and lakes? Take a look!
## See if you can find the animals in the picture.

Which animal is a fish?

Which animal can fly?

Which animal can hop?

Which animal carries its home on its back?

# PIPE-CLEANER CATTAILS

Cattails are hard to miss. They can grow very tall, and they have a soft, velvety brown "tail" at the top. This brown tail is actually part of the plant's flower. What are flowers like that you usually see?

## WHAT YOU NEED:

- Construction paper (any light color)
- Green marker
- Child safety scissors
- Brown pipe cleaners
- Craft glue

## WHAT YOU DO:

**1.** Hold the paper vertically, like a piece of writing paper. Draw tall stems and leaves on the paper with a green marker. Leave a space at the top of the paper.

**2.** Cut the pipe cleaner into 2" (5 cm) pieces.

**3.** Glue the pipe cleaners to the top of the stems for cattails.

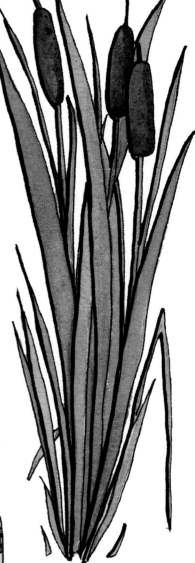

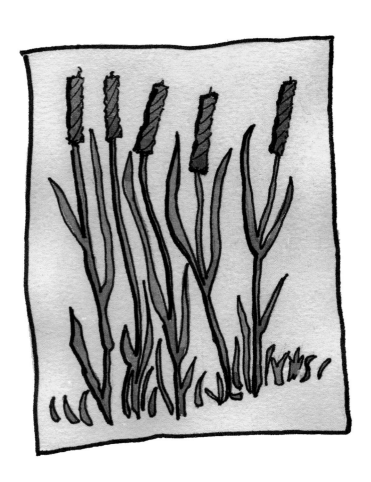

## FIELD NOTES

Cattails can grow in most places where there is water, like ponds. They can also grow in wetlands, or even in ditches that have water. You can sometimes spot cattails growing along roadways.

## WHAT'S IN A NAME?

What do you imagine when you hear the name *cattail*? What does this name tell you about the plant? Think of other plant names you know. How do the plant names tell you about the plant? For example, what do you imagine when you hear the plant names *bluebell* or *buttercup*?

☞ **TRY THIS!** Look for cattails the next time you drive someplace with your family. Draw and write your own field notes to tell where you saw the cattails.

### Art Lesson

• Do you have any leftover pipe cleaners? Think about an animal the pipe cleaner could be. Glue the pipe cleaner to construction paper. Draw in legs, a tail, ears, and other animal features to bring your pipe-cleaner animal to life.

# CLOTHESPIN SNAPPING TURTLE

Turtles are members of the reptile family. The snapping turtle is a very good swimmer. What is something that you are very good at doing?

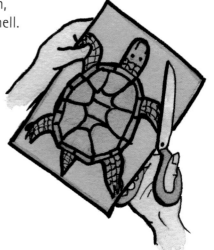

## WHAT YOU NEED:

- Black marker, pencil, or crayon
- Green construction paper
- Child safety scissors
- Clip-type clothespin
- Glue stick

## WHAT YOU DO:

**1.** Draw a turtle on green construction paper. Draw on eyes, a mouth, and a pattern on its shell.

**2.** Cut out the turtle.

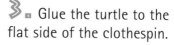

**3.** Glue the turtle to the flat side of the clothespin.

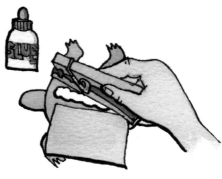

**4.** Open and close the clothespin to make the turtle "snap."

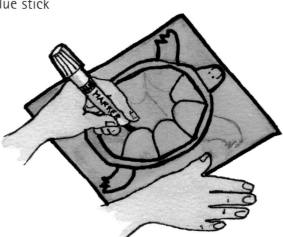

## WORDS TO KNOW

The common snapping turtle is *nocturnal*. *Nocturnal* means to be active at night. So a snapping turtle is mostly active at night! What do you do at night? Are you mostly active, or do you mostly sleep?

The snapping turtle cannot pull itself into its shell. It moves very slowly on dry land. It defends itself by biting. When threatened, the snapping turtle lunges forward and bites. It also uses its strong jaw to catch its food. Snapping turtles like to eat plants, fish, frogs, even small mammals (like mice) and small birds!

## Art Lesson
- Draw pictures of foods a snapping turtle might eat. Cut them out. Place the food drawings in the mouth of your clothespin snapping turtle.

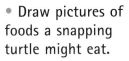

## LOOK AND LISTEN

The common snapping turtle, like all turtles, has no vocal cords. It can only make hissing and grunting sounds! Try making turtle noises. Try making these sounds without moving your lips.

☞ **TRY THIS!** Use your clothespin snapping turtle to hold your school papers and drawings.

# TWIG BEAVER DAM

Beavers are excellent builders. They build lodges out of sticks and mud. What material was used to build your home? Do you see bricks, concrete, stones, or wood on the outside of your home?

## WHAT YOU NEED:

- Cereal box cardboard
- Child safety scissors
- Glue stick
- Blue construction paper
- Dry, thin twigs
- Liquid glue
- Marker

## WHAT YOU DO:

**1.** Cut off one big side of a cereal box.

**2.** With a glue stick, glue blue construction paper to the cereal-box cardboard. Cut away any extra paper.

**3.** Break the twigs into small pieces. With liquid glue, glue the twigs to one corner of the cardboard. This will be the beaver dam.

**4.** Draw the bank of the river. Draw in some plants and some river water. You might also draw a beaver's tail sticking out of the dam!

## WORDS TO KNOW

Young beavers are called *kits*.

☛ **TRY THIS!** Beavers have to swim underwater to enter their lodge. They are strong swimmers and are able to remain under water for up to 15 minutes. That means that they hold their breath for 15 minutes! How long can you hold your breath? Ask an adult to count how many seconds you hold your breath. Figure out how much longer a beaver can holds its breath than you can. Why do you think it's important for a beaver to be able to hold its breath?

## FIELD NOTES

A beaver dam and a beaver lodge are not the same thing. The dam is a structure that blocks the flow of water. The lodge is the actual place where the beaver lives. Beavers build their dams upstream from where they build their lodges. The dam forms a deep pond that won't freeze in winter. This is important. If the water froze, the beavers would not be able to get inside their lodges. Now their lodges can be used all year long! In what ways does your home change with the seasons?

**Little Hands Story Corner™**

Read *Get Busy, Beaver!* by Carolyn Crimi.

# PLASTIC-STRAW DRAGONFLY

Dragonflies are insects. Ponds are important to dragonflies because dragonflies lay their eggs here. The eggs hatch underwater, and the young dragonflies, called nymphs, live underwater. When they become adults, they grow wings and leave the pond. But they never go too far!

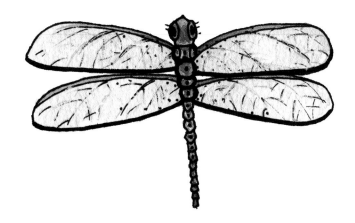

## WHAT YOU NEED:

- Wax paper
- Pen
- Child safety scissors
- Glue
- Plastic drinking straw
- 2 Pony beads*

## WHAT YOU DO:

**1.** First create the dragonfly's wings. Draw the wings on waxed paper. Draw veins on the wings, too.

**2.** Cut out the wings.

**3.** Glue the wings to the straw.

**4.** Glue pony beads on one end of the straw. These are the dragonfly's eyes.

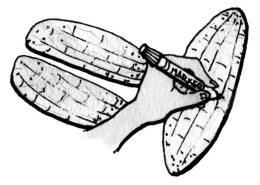

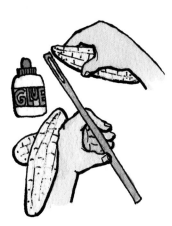

\* **Warning!** Small beads pose a choking danger to young children. Grown-ups should control the supply and insert them into the project.

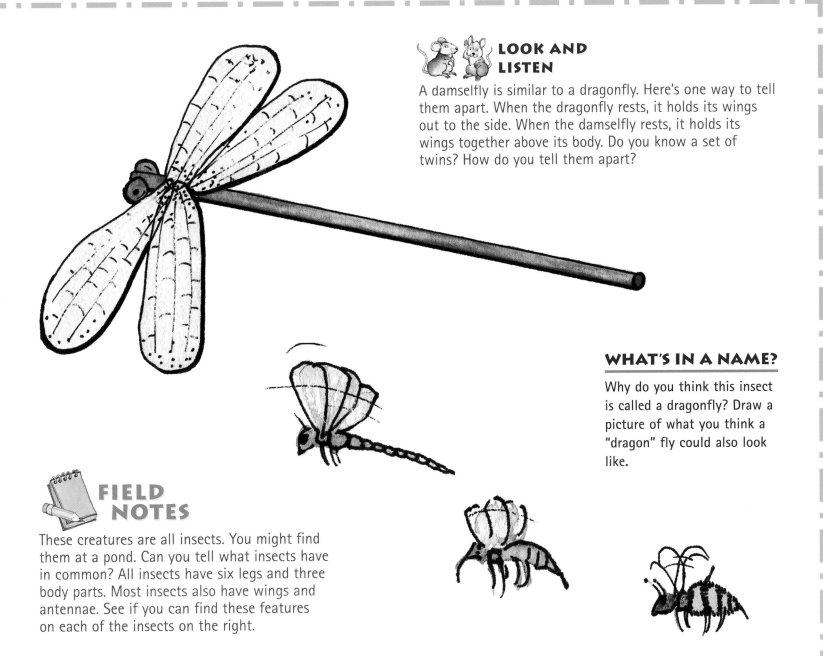

A damselfly is similar to a dragonfly. Here's one way to tell them apart. When the dragonfly rests, it holds its wings out to the side. When the damselfly rests, it holds its wings together above its body. Do you know a set of twins? How do you tell them apart?

## WHAT'S IN A NAME?

Why do you think this insect is called a dragonfly? Draw a picture of what you think a "dragon" fly could also look like.

## FIELD NOTES

These creatures are all insects. You might find them at a pond. Can you tell what insects have in common? All insects have six legs and three body parts. Most insects also have wings and antennae. See if you can find these features on each of the insects on the right.

# FINGER-PUPPET BULLFROG

A bullfrog is an amphibian. An amphibian is an animal that spends part of its life in the water, and part of its life on land. Which part do you think a bullfrog spends in the water—as a young frog or as a grown-up? Which part does it spend on land?

**WHAT YOU NEED:**

- Green or brown construction paper
- Dark marker or crayon
- Child safety scissors
- Green and brown poster paint
- Shallow dish
- Clean household sponge
- Transparent tape

**WHAT YOU DO:**

**1.** Draw a frog on the construction paper. Cut it out.

**2.** Pour some paint into a shallow dish. Dip the sponge into the paint, then dab the paint onto the frog. Allow the paint to dry.

**3.** Measure and cut a strip of construction paper, 1" x 3" (2.5 cm x 2.5 cm). Tape the ends of the strip together so you've made a circle.

**4.** Tape the circle to the back of the frog cutout.

**5.** Slip your finger inside the circle. Move your finger to move your bullfrog puppet.

## LOOK AND LISTEN

A bullfrog is a kind, or a species, of frog. Each frog species makes its own unique sound that only the female of the same species responds to. The bullfrog gets its name from its powerful sound, or call. It sounds more like the bellow of a bull than the croak of a frog! Try it! Croak like you imagine a frog croaks. Then bellow like you imagine a bull would bellow. Make another puppet, and hold a conversation between two bellowing bullfrogs.

## FIELD NOTES

Bullfrogs are born underwater. They hatch from eggs that lay in the pond. A young frog is called a tadpole. Tadpoles can't breathe air. They have gills, like a fish, that help them breathe underwater. As the tadpole grows, its body changes. The tadpole starts to grow legs, and its gills close up. The tadpole has become a frog! How will you change as you grow up?

☞ **TRY THIS!** Bullfrogs are excellent jumpers. Their webbed feet and strong, muscular back legs help them jump. A bullfrog can jump 3 to 6 feet (1 to 2 m). Get a tape measure. Measure how far a frog can jump. Now see if you can jump as far as a frog. Use the tape measure to see how far you can leap.

# SALMON FLIP BOOK

Salmon are fish that live part of their lives in rivers and part of their lives in the ocean. Most salmon live in cooler areas of North America, like Alaska, Canada, and the northeastern United States.

**WHAT YOU NEED:**

- Dark marker
- Scrap of lightweight cardboard
- Child safety scissors
- Pad of white paper or self-stick notes
- Colored markers or crayons

**WHAT YOU DO:**

**1.** Draw the shape of a salmon on lightweight cardboard, and cut it out. This cardboard salmon will be the pattern for your flip book.

**2.** Trace the head of the salmon on the first page of the pad of self-stick notes.

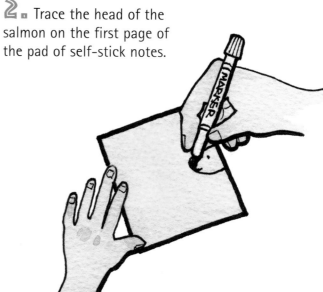

**3.** Trace the salmon on each page, moving it forward slightly each time. Continue until the salmon "swims" off the page.

**4.** Add details to your salmon. Make sure the salmon on each page is colored the same and has the same details.

**5.** Hold the pad in one hand and flip with the other. Watch as the salmon "swims" across the page.

☛ **TRY THIS!** After being out at sea, salmon return to the rivers in which they were born. They find their way back home by following their noses. Salmon are able to smell the scent of their home streams. They will follow the river, swimming against the river's flow. How do you find your way back home? Do you travel with a friend who knows the way? Do you read street signs? Which buildings and landmarks do you recognize? Draw the things that help you find your way home.

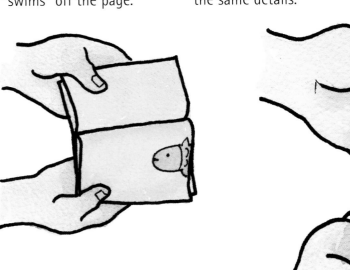

### FIELD NOTES

There are many different kinds, or species, of salmon. Most salmon are born in rivers. They may live in the river for a few years while they grow, or mature. They will then follow the river until it ends at the ocean. They may live in the ocean for many years. Salmon in the northeastern part of North America live in the North Atlantic Ocean. Salmon that live in the northwestern part of North America live in the North Pacific Ocean. Look at a map. Find the oceans. Try to trace the river routes the salmon might swim.

# Welcome to the Seashore!

Close your eyes, and imagine a beach. Even if you have never been to a beach, think of beaches you have seen on TV or in pictures. Imagine the sand squishing between your toes. Imagine the water tickling your feet. Imagine the sound of the waves as they crash on the shore. And do you hear that "cawing" sound? That's the sound of a gull. Many people enjoy going to the beach to swim and to build sandcastles and to lie in the sun.

The beach is more than just a place for people to enjoy. The beach, or the seashore, is a habitat, too. Tiny animals burrow in the sand. Shorebirds, like gulls, search for a tasty meal. Plants bow to the wind and salty sea spray. Not all seashores are sandy. Some are rocky, and others have both rocks and sand.

## What do all seashores have in common?

All seashores are where the sea and the land meet.

All seashores change from the movement of the water and the wind.

If you were to visit a seashore, you might want to bring back a souvenir. You can make your own seashore souvenirs here! As you make seashore prints and the other projects in this chapter, you'll discover the world where the land meets the sea.

What might you find if you visited a seashore?
Take a look! Imagine you are on a seashore treasure hunt.
See which treasures you can find in the picture.

Try to find an animal that can fly.

Try to find an animal that has a claw for a hand.

Try to find an animal with eight legs.

Try to find an object in which an animal once lived.

# STYROFOAM TRAY SEASHORE PRINT

Some seashores are sandy, others are rocky, and some seashores are in between. A tiny grain of sand was once a much larger rock. As the rock traveled in the water, it broke apart and became smaller. Eventually, the rock became a grain of sand on a beach. You might also see sand along a river or a lake. Where have you seen sand?

## WHAT YOU NEED:

- Styrofoam tray, from fruits or vegetables*
- Child safety scissors
- Pencil with a dull point
- Newspaper to protect surfaces
- Tempera paint (any color)
- Paintbrush
- White paper

## WHAT YOU DO:

**1.** Cut away the sides of the Styrofoam tray so the tray is flat.

**2.** Draw pictures of seashore creatures on the tray. Use a pencil with a dull point. Be sure to press down hard with your pencil so you've made a deep crease for the outline of your picture.

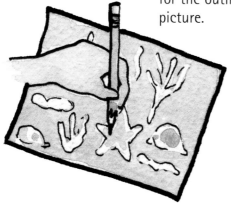

**3.** Spread newspaper on the tabletop to protect the table's surface. Then lightly brush paint over the tray. (If you apply too much paint, it will fill the pencil creases. Try not to fill the creases.)

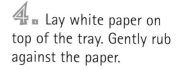

**4.** Lay white paper on top of the tray. Gently rub against the paper.

**5.** Lift the paper. Your seashore print will be on the bottom side.

* Caution: Do not use Styrofoam trays from meat packages. The meat juice could leave behind bacteria that might make you sick.

☛ **TRY THIS!** Make prints in three different colors. Place each print, one above the other, to show three zones of the seashore.

☛ **TRY THIS, TOO!** Create a beach scene! Pour a thin layer of oatmeal or cornmeal in the bottom of a baking pan with raised sides. This is the "sand" of your seashore. Add dried pasta shells, small toy sea creatures, and smooth stones. Use foil for water. You might also add the animals you make in the next projects to your seashore habitat.

## FIELD NOTES

The seashore has three distinct areas, or zones, where plants and animals live.

- Plants and animals that live in the **high intertidal zone** are exposed to rough waves and long periods of time outside the water.
- Next is the **middle intertidal zone**, which is either fully covered or fully uncovered by water every day. When the tide is out (or low), the plants and animals that live here are exposed to the air. When the tide is in (or high), the plants and animals are covered with water.
- The third zone is the **low intertidal zone**. This zone is mostly covered by water at almost all times. This zone is exposed to air only during the lowest tides.

**Little Hands Story Corner™**

Read *Gramma's Walk* by Anna Grossnickle Hines.

# PAPER HERRING GULL

Herring gulls are the most common kind of gull at the seashore. They are scavenger birds. That means that they look for food leftover from other animals—even from people! Gulls play an important role in cleaning up beaches and harbors. Sometimes they even visit garbage dumps, searching for food. What might the seashore look like if gulls didn't live there?

## WHAT YOU NEED:

- White paper, like white typing or copier paper
- Pencil
- Child safety scissors
- Black and yellow crayons
- Glue
- Pipe cleaner

## WHAT YOU DO:

**1.** Fold the white paper in half so it resembles a card shape.

**2.** Draw one bird's wing on one side of the folded paper. Keep the wide end of the wing along the folded line.

**3.** Cut out the wing, cutting both halves of the paper. Don't cut the fold line. When you unfold the paper, you will have two connected wings.

**4.** From the remaining paper, draw and cut out the shape of the bird's body.

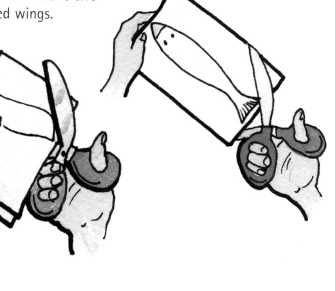

**5.** Color the edges of the wings black. Color the gull's tail black, too. Color its beak yellow.

**6.** Glue the gull's body to the center of the wing.

**7.** Poke the tip of a pipe cleaner through the center of the gull. Twist the end of the pipe cleaner to hold it in place.

**8.** Wiggle the end of the pipe cleaner to make the gull "fly."

## LOOK AND LISTEN

Herring gulls are noisy birds. They sound like loud wails or laughs. What do you think the gulls might be laughing at? Next time you visit the seashore listen to the gulls. What do you think they sound like?

## FIELD NOTES

Herring gulls like to eat animals that live in shells, like oysters and clams. How do the gulls get to the animals inside the shells? They pick up the shellfish, fly into the air with them, then drop the shellfish from the air onto a hard surface, like a rock. Hopefully, the shells crack open, and the gulls eat the meat inside.

## Art Lesson

• Make several paper gulls and tape string or yarn to each one. Attach the strings at different heights to a clothes hanger for a herring gull mobile.

☛ **TRY THIS!** What foods do you know that come in shells? How about a peanut or a walnut? How do you crack open a nut in its shell? Do you use your fingers or a nutcracker? Try opening a food in a shell. Imagine you didn't have hands, like the herring gull.

# EGG-CARTON FIDDLER CRAB

Animals that live at the seashore hide from waves by crawling under or between rocks or plants. Crabs crawl into crevices or cracks in rocks. If you visit a seashore, you might find a crab hiding in the crevices of rocks.

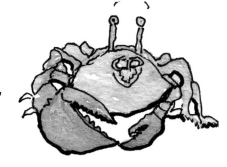

## WHAT YOU NEED:

- Styrofoam egg carton
- Child safety scissors
- Pipe cleaners
- Pencil
- Scrap of red construction paper
- White craft glue

## WHAT YOU DO:

**1.** Cut one cup from the egg carton. This will be the crab's body.

**2.** Cut two pipe cleaners into eight equal pieces, about 2 inches (5 cm) long.

**3.** Poke four pipe-cleaner pieces into each side of the egg-carton cup, near the bottom. These will be the crab's legs.

**4.** Cut two more 2-inch pipe-cleaner pieces.

**5.** Draw and cut out two claws from red paper.

## WORDS TO KNOW

*Crustaceans* are arthropods. Arthropods have exoskeletons—skeletons that surround their bodies, like a hard protective shell. (Humans and other animals have skeletons inside their bodies.) Insects are arthropods, too. Along with an exoskeleton, crustaceans usually have several pairs of jointed legs, antennae, and eyes at the ends of stalks.

**6.** Glue each claw to the new pipe-cleaner pieces. Poke the ends of these pieces to the "front" of the egg-carton cup.

**7.** Cut two more 2-inch pipe-cleaner pieces.

**8.** Poke them through the top of the egg-carton cup. These are the "stalks" on top of which sit the crab's eyes.

 **LOOK AND LISTEN**

Visit this website to see a fiddler crab scurry across the sand: http://pelotes.jea.com/fidcrab.htm

 **FIELD NOTES**

The male fiddler crab has one claw that is larger than the other. The male crab waves its oversized claw up and down to attract the attention of females or to fight other males. Compare the length of your fingers. Is one finger longer than the others? Is one finger shorter?

 **Art Lesson**

• Make lots of different animals using egg carton cups. The best animals are ones you make up!

# CARDBOARD-TUBE TWO-SPOTTED OCTOPUS

Octopus are not fish, and they're not crustaceans (like crabs). In fact, octopus have no bones in their bodies! Their bodies are very soft. They belong to the mollusk family. Other animals in the mollusk family are oysters, clams, and squid. An octopus is well known for its eight arms, or tentacles.

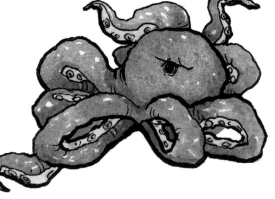

## WHAT YOU NEED:

- Cardboard tube
- Child safety scissors
- Brown, blue, and white crayons
- Black marker
- Black construction paper
- Glue or tape
- Pencil

## WORDS TO KNOW

An octopus den (or home) is called a *midden*. Octopus like to eat shellfish. They are very tidy eaters. They leave neat piles of shells outside their middens.

## WHAT YOU DO:

**1.** Cut a 2-inch (5 cm) section from the cardboard tube.

**2.** Color the cardboard tube brown. This is the octopus's body. Draw eyes on the tube, too. Also draw two blue circles under the eyes. (These spots are how this octopus got its name.)

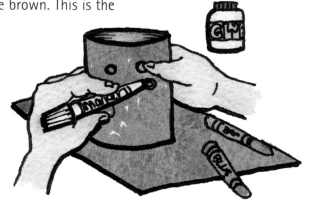

**3.** Cut out eight octopus arms from black construction paper. (See the picture for the shape of the arms.)

**4.** Draw white suction cups on each arm.

**5.** Tape or glue the arms inside the tube, at the bottom of your octopus's face. Make sure the white spots are facing down.

**6.** Roll each octopus arm around a pencil. Hold it there briefly, then unroll. Your octopus arms will curve upward, like they are waving in the water.

## SEASHORE SCIENCE

Octopus can confuse their enemies by squirting a cloud of ink. Fill a glass with water. Place a heavy object, such as a rock, in the bottom of the glass. Is it easy to see the rock through the water? Now squirt a few drops of blue food coloring in the water. How clearly do you see the rock now?

## WHAT'S IN A NAME?

Seastars also live at the seashore. What do you think a seastar looks like? Look at the shapes below. Point to the one that you think is the seastar.

## FIELD NOTES

One way an octopus moves is by filling a cavity (an open space) in its body with water, then shooting out the water. The shooting water propels—or moves—the octopus very quickly. How might you move quickly through water?

# Welcome to the Arctic Tundra!

Have you ever been cold? Really, really cold? What did you do to warm up? Maybe you put on a sweater. Perhaps you put on a thick coat to go outside. You wore mittens to protect your hands and a hat to keep your head warm. If it had snowed, you might wear boots to keep your feet warm. The bottoms of the boots probably also stop you from slipping on the ice.

Animals and plants that live in very cold habitats adapt so they stay warm, too. One of the coldest habitats in North America is the Arctic tundra. The Arctic tundra lies across parts of Alaska and Canada. The tundra ground is covered by a thin layer of soil. Plants grow here in the spring. Beneath this layer lies a layer of ice, called permafrost. This ice never melts.

## What makes the tundra special?

The tundra does not have tall plants.

The tundra has a short summer and a long winter.

Even though the tundra might seem like a cold, lifeless place, it is actually teeming with life. The tundra also has a nighttime show you won't want to miss. So pull on your parka and get out your boots. It's time to trek across the tundra of North America!

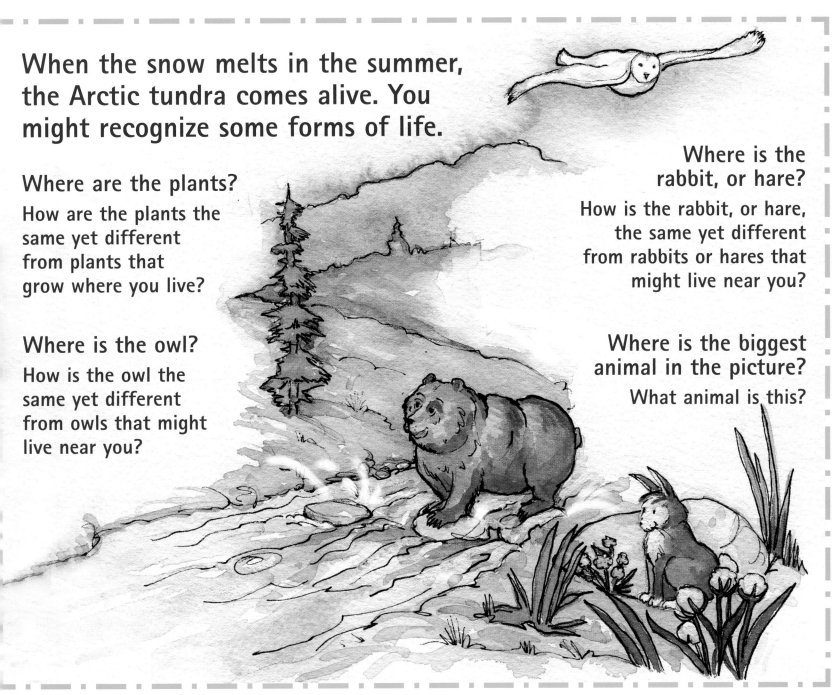

When the snow melts in the summer, the Arctic tundra comes alive. You might recognize some forms of life.

**Where are the plants?**

How are the plants the same yet different from plants that grow where you live?

**Where is the owl?**

How is the owl the same yet different from owls that might live near you?

**Where is the rabbit, or hare?**

How is the rabbit, or hare, the same yet different from rabbits or hares that might live near you?

**Where is the biggest animal in the picture?**

What animal is this?

# SUMMER/WINTER SNOWSHOE HARE

Snowshoe hares are masters at camouflage. Camouflage is an animal's ability to blend in with its surroundings. In the winter, the snowshoe hare's fur is white. In the summer, the hare's fur is brown. Why do you think white and brown are good winter/summer colors for the snowshoe hare? Complete the project to find out!

Which snowshoe hare is wearing its winter colors?
Which is wearing its summer colors?

## WHAT YOU NEED:

- Sheet of white construction paper
- Sheet of brown construction paper
- Glue stick
- White tempera paint, in a dish or lid
- Brown tempera paint, in a dish or lid
- Thin black marker or pen

## WHAT YOU DO:

**1.** Glue the brown and white sheets of paper together, back to back.

**2.** Dip your thumb in the white paint, and press your thumb to the white paper. This is the body of the snowshoe hare in winter.

**3.** To make the hare's head, dip the tip of your pointer finger into the white paint, then press your finger slightly above the thumbprint, but still connected to it. Allow the paint to dry.

**4.** Once the paint has dried, turn the paper over to the brown side. Repeat Steps 2 and 3, using brown paint. This is the snowshoe hare in summer.

**5.** With the marker or pen, draw the hare's ears, legs, tail, eyes, nose and whiskers on both sides of the paper.

**Snowshoe hare in summer.**

**Snowshoe hare in winter.**

## FIELD NOTES

Did you figure out why white is a good winter color for the snowshoe hare, and why brown is a good summer color? In the winter, the hare's white color helps it blend in with the snow. In the summer, the hare's brown color helps it blend in with the brown tundra landscape. Blending in, or camouflaging, helps the snowshoe hare hide from predators—animals that might want to eat it. What do you wear in summer or in winter? How do your clothes help you each season?

☞ **TRY THIS!** Another way that snowshoe hares often "hide" from predators is by freezing. Young hares often "freeze" in their tracks when they sense danger. By freezing, they hope that the predator won't see or notice them. Play a game of "statue." Choose one player to be the "sculptor," while the other players are "statues." The sculptor twirls each player around and tells him or her to "freeze" in a pose. When each player has been frozen, the sculptor picks his or her favorite pose, and that player is the next sculptor.

### WORDS TO KNOW
*Tundra* comes from the country of Finland. In the Finnish language, the word *tunturia* means "treeless plain."

**Little Hands Story Corner™**

Read *Hello, Arctic!* by Theodore Taylor.

# SNOWY OWL SOCK PUPPET

The snowy owl is one of the predators of the Arctic tundra. That means that the snowy owl hunts other animals for food. It hunts during the day, snatching small prey with its talons, or feet, as it flies. Small birds, mice, and snowshoe hares are often on the snowy owl's menu. What do you think of when you hear the word *owl*?

## WHAT YOU NEED:

- White athletic sock
- Fabric scissors
- Fabric or craft glue
- Scrap of yellow felt or paper
- Wiggly eyes*

## WHAT YOU DO:

**1.** Cut off the sock's ribbing. The foot of the sock will be the owl's body.

**2.** From the ribbing, cut out two wing shapes. Glue the wings to the side of the foot of the sock.

**3.** From yellow felt, cut out a beak shape. Glue the beak to the front of the sock.

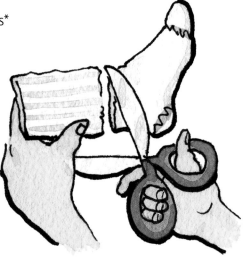

*Warning! Small beads pose a choking danger to young children. Grown-ups should control the supply and insert them into the project.

**4.** Glue wiggly eyes above the beak.

**5.** Place your hand inside the sock for a puppet.

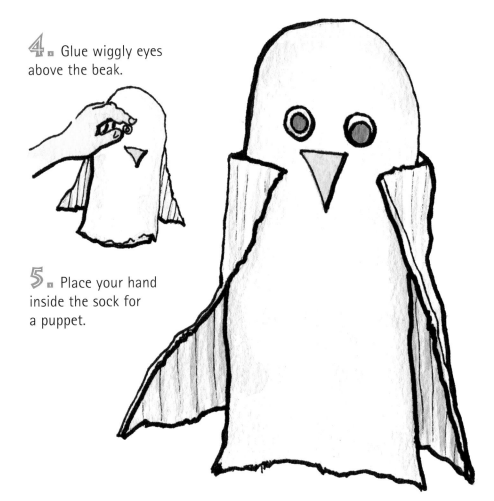

## FIELD NOTES

The snowy owl's large eyes and flexible neck allow it to see all around. The owl can turn its head up to 270 degrees to see in either direction. (If it could turn its head completely around, that would be 360 degrees.) How do you think this ability helps the snowy owl as a hunter?

☛ **TRY THIS!** Can you turn your head as far as a snowy owl? Try it! How far can you turn your head? What do you see in each direction? Why is it not as important for people to be able to turn their heads as far as the snowy owl can?

## Art Lesson

• Make other sock-puppet animals using scraps of fabric, yarn, and wiggly eyes. Then put on a puppet show.

## LOOK AND LISTEN

Snowy owls communicate with each other with a series of shrieks and hoots. Make a code of shrieks and hoots with your friends. Shriek and hoot to communicate with each other.

# PAINTED NORTHERN LIGHTS

An amazing sight can sometimes be seen in the sky in northern areas, like those of the Arctic. It is the northern lights. The northern lights are flashing, dancing colors that swirl across the sky. These lights are only seen in polar areas. Southern lights are also seen around the Antarctic, around the South Pole. To create your own northern lights, follow the directions.

## WHAT YOU NEED:

- Newspaper
- Wax paper
- Tempera paint (red, yellow, blue, white)
- Popsicle stick
- Glue stick
- Blue construction paper

## WORDS TO KNOW

*Aurora Borealis* is another name for the northern lights. The southern lights are called *aurora australis.* Label the picture you make with your own name for the northern lights.

## WHAT YOU DO:

**1.** Cover a table with newspaper to protect the table's surface.

**2.** Lay a sheet of wax paper on the newspaper.

**3.** Squeeze a few drops of paint onto the wax paper. Use drops of different colors.

**4.** Lay a second sheet of wax paper over the paint drops.

**5.** Spread the paint in between the wax sheets of paper, moving the Popsicle stick across the top of the paper, back and forth. Allow the paint to dry. The pages should stick together. (You might glue any open corners or edges with a glue stick.)

**6.** Glue the wax paper onto medium- or dark-blue construction paper for a colored background.

## FIELD NOTES

The beautiful blaze of the northern lights, or aurora borealis, is formed by hot winds that come from the sun, or solar winds. The winds light up tiny particles in the air, which reflect the sun's light. Look up at the nighttime sky where you live. What do you see? Can you see constellations—groupings of stars? Do you see individual stars, the moon, even the planets?

## LOOK AND LISTEN

Check out this web site to see the northern lights:
http://www.exploratorium.edu/learning_studio/auroras/auroraslook.html

# MILK-CARTON GRIZZLY BEAR

Two types of bears live on the Arctic tundra. One is the brown bear, also called a grizzly bear. Adult grizzly bears are very large. They can grow to be 5 to 8 feet (1.5 to 2.5 m) tall!

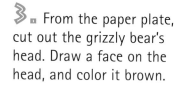

## WORDS TO KNOW

Brown bears spend much of the winter in a state of deep sleep, or *hibernation*. They sleep during the winter because food is hard to find at that time. Sleeping requires less energy than being awake, so the bears don't need to eat during the winter. Also, their bodies store a lot of fat from the food they ate during the warmer seasons. The bear's body burns this fat for energy while the bear hibernates. How do your habits change with the seasons?

## WHAT YOU NEED:

- Brown paper lunch bag
- Child safety scissors
- Dry, clean milk carton, quart-size
- Transparent tape
- Small white paper plate
- Black marker
- Brown crayon
- Glue

## WHAT YOU DO:

**1.** Cut open a brown paper lunch bag so it lies flat in one big piece.

**2.** Wrap the paper around a dry, clean, quart-size milk carton, and tape the paper in place. This will be the body of your grizzly bear.

**3.** From the paper plate, cut out the grizzly bear's head. Draw a face on the head, and color it brown.

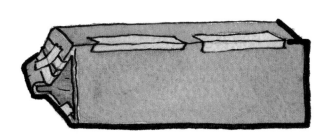

**4.** From the rim of the paper plate, cut out the bear's ears, legs, and arms. Draw details on the ears, legs, and arms, and color them brown, too.

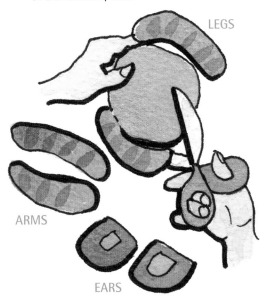

LEGS

ARMS

EARS

**5.** Glue the ears to the top of the grizzly-bear head.

**6.** Glue the head, arms, and legs to the front of the milk carton.

# FIELD NOTES

Some animals only eat plants, and some animals only eat other animals. Grizzly bears eat both plants *and* animals! Grizzly bears eat plants, like berries, nuts, roots, and leaves. They also eat animals, like fish. How is a grizzly bear's diet similar to your own? How is it different?

☛**TRY THIS!** **Brown bears are also called grizzly bears because of the outer hairs on their furry coats. These outer hairs are tipped with a white or silver color, giving the bear a "grizzled" look. Use a white crayon to give your milk-carton grizzly bear a grizzled look.**

**Little Hands Story Corner™**

Read *Grizzly Bear Family Book* by Michio Hoshino.

# SHOE-BOX POLAR BEAR PAWS

Polar bears are the second type of bear you might find on the Arctic tundra. The North Pole is surrounded by the Arctic Ocean, not land. The ocean is frozen and covered by large sheets of ice, or ice floes. Polar bears are most comfortable on the ice or swimming in the cold water of the Arctic Ocean.

## WHAT YOU NEED:

- Two shoe boxes, with lids
- Transparent tape
- White paper
- Regular scissors (ask a grown-up to help)
- Scrap of black construction paper
- Child safety scissors

## WORDS TO KNOW

*Nanuk* means "polar bear" in the Inuktitut language. The Inuktitut are a Native American group.

## WHAT YOU DO:

**1.** Place the lids on the shoe boxes and tape them down.

**2.** Wrap each shoe box in white paper, and tape the paper in place.

**3.** Have a grown-up cut a hole in the center of each box lid, big enough to fit your foot inside.

**4.** Cut out ten polar-bear claws from black construction paper—five for each shoe box. Glue the claws to the front of each shoe box.

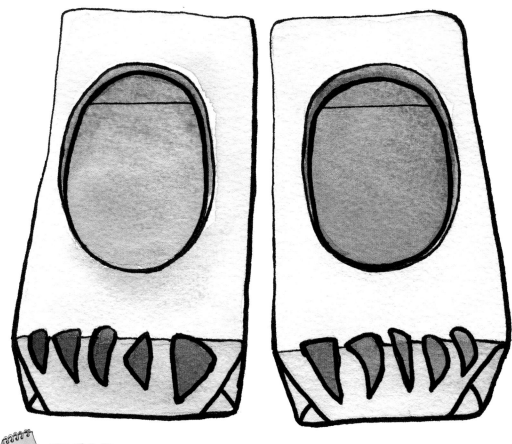

Polar bears are as much at home in the ocean as they are on land. They often live near the coast, which is the perfect place for the polar bears to hunt one of their favorite foods, seals. When swimming under ice floes, the bears come up for air at breathing holes.

How does the Arctic Ocean feel? Find out! Fill a plastic glass or cup with water. Dip your finger in the water. Is the water warm or cool? Add a few ice cubes to the water. How did the ice change the water's temperature? Is the water warmer or cooler?

## FIELD NOTES

A polar bear's paws are perfect for living in the Arctic. The bear's claws prevent the polar bear from slipping across the ice and snow, and the fur on its paws keep the bear's paws warm.

☞ **TRY THIS!** What do you wear on your feet so they stay warm and dry? How do your shoes or sneakers help you walk? Wear your shoe-box polar-bear paws and "pad" around your room. Imagine you're a polar bear, roaming across an ice floe in the cold Arctic.

**Little Hands Story Corner™**

Read *Polar Bear, Polar Bear, What Do You Hear?* by Bill Martin, Jr., Eric Carle (illustrator).

# Welcome to the Grasslands!

What are fields of grass like where you live? Perhaps you have a grassy field at your school for playing sports. Maybe your local park has grassy fields for picnics. Think about how the grass feels on your hands. How does it feel as you walk or run across it? What does the grass look like and smell like?

A grass is a type of plant, and grasslands are habitats covered mostly with grass. Sometimes they have a few trees and bushes, but mostly the grass stretches as far as you can see. In different places grasslands have different names. In Africa, they're called savannahs. In Asia, they're called steppes. In South America, they're called pampas. Here in North America grasslands are called prairies.

## What do all grasslands have in common?

All grasslands are mostly flat.

The main plant of grasslands is grass.

In North America, the prairies are sometimes called "vanishing grasslands." The rich prairie soil is used for farming, and cities have sprouted where the grasses once grew. Still, many areas in central North America are covered by grasslands. Let's see who lives here!

Some animals that live on the prairie hide among the prairie's tall grasses. Others you can see right away. Which prairie animals can you find?

**Where is the pronghorn antelope?** (Hint: It has horns!)

**Where is the prairie dog?** (Hint: It looks more like a big squirrel than a dog!)

**Where is the bison?** (Hint: It is the biggest animal of the prairie!)

**Where is the caterpillar?** (Hint: It is yellow, white, and black!)

# PAPER PRAIRIE

What do you think the most important plant on the prairie is? That's right—grass! Grasses don't need a lot of water to grow, but they do need a lot of sunshine. That's why most grasslands occur in between mountains, deserts, and forests—places that get enough water, but that do not have very many trees. (Trees block the sunlight.) What is the grass like where you live? What does it need to stay green and healthy?

## WHAT YOU NEED:

- Green construction paper
- Child safety scissors
- Glue stick
- Blue construction paper
- Pencil with eraser
- Red and yellow tempera paint, in a dish or lid

## WHAT YOU DO:

**1.** Cut three long strips of green construction paper, about 2 inches (5 cm) wide.

**2.** Cut fringe on one long side of each strip.

**3.** Glue one strip of green construction paper to the bottom edge of the blue construction paper. *Don't glue down the fringe.*

**4.** Position the next strip of green construction paper behind the fringe of the first strip. Glue it into place, but again, *do not glue down the fringe.*

**5.** Position the last strip of green construction paper behind the fringe of the second strip. Glue it into place, too, but *do not glue down the fringe.*

**6.** Dip the pencil eraser into the red and/or yellow paint, and dab the eraser to the green paper for flowers.

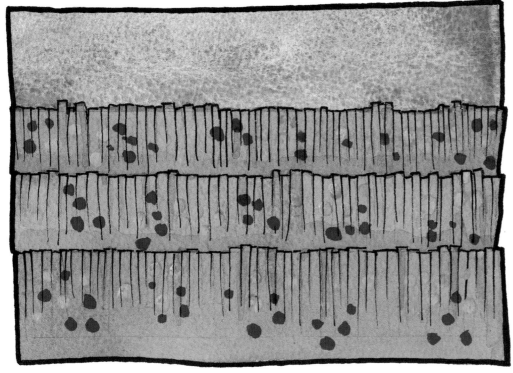

 **LOOK AND LISTEN**

Check out this website about grasslands and prairies:
http://mbgnet.mobot.org/sets/grasslnd/main.htm

 **FIELD NOTES**

Do you like to eat cereal? The cereal that farmers grow for food comes from wild grasses! Get a box of cereal and find the list of ingredients. Look for words like *oats, wheat,* or *rye*. These plants are types of cereal grasses! Many prairies in the United States are owned by farmers, who grow and harvest cereal grasses for us to eat.

## WHAT'S IN A NAME?

Here are some of the plants that grow on the prairie: big bluestem, little bluestem, butterfly weed, and purple coneflower. Think about the names of these plants. What do you think the plants look like? Draw pictures of these plants on your paper prairie.

 **Little Hands Story Corner™**

Read *A Tallgrass Prairie Alphabet* by Claudia McGhee.

# POP-UP PRAIRIE DOG

Prairie dogs build elaborate burrows, called "towns," under the ground. The burrow has rooms for sleeping, to store food, even to "go to the bathroom"! Over 1,000 prairie dogs can live in a prairie-dog town. Prairie dogs poke up from holes in the ground to check out what is happening on the prairie and to get food. Why do you leave your home?

## WHAT YOU NEED:

- Paper drinking cup
- Regular scissors (ask a grown-up to help)
- White craft glue
- Brown paper lunch bag
- Brown construction paper
- Black marker
- Popsicle stick

## WHAT YOU DO:

**1.** Cut a slit in the bottom of the paper cup. Ask a parent if you need help.

**2.** Spread glue around the outside of the cup.

**3.** Wrap brown paper, cut from a lunch bag, around the cup. Cut away any excess paper, too.

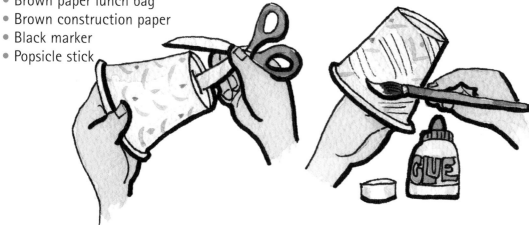

## WORDS TO KNOW

A family of black-tailed prairie dogs is called a *coterie*. Coteries usually have an adult male, three or four adult females, and a few babies. Who are the people that make up your family?

**4.** On brown construction paper, draw the top half a prairie dog, like the one shown here. Draw features on the prairie dog's face, too.

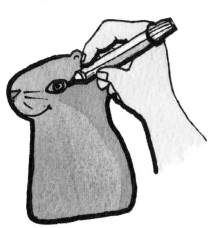

**5.** Cut out the prairie dog, and glue it to the end of the Popsicle stick.

**6.** Put the Popsicle stick inside the cup, and poke the end through the slit cut into the cup's bottom. The stick should poke through the bottom of the cup.

**7.** Move the stick up and down through the slit to see the prairie dog pop up from its burrow.

 **LOOK AND LISTEN**

Prairie dogs make a high-pitched barking sound. They make this sound to tell other prairie dogs that danger is near. Scientists think prairie dogs have a complex communication system. Check out this web site to learn more about prairie dogs: http://www.desertusa.com/dec96/du_pdogs.html

 **FIELD NOTES**

Prairie dogs recognize each other by kissing and wagging their tails. How do you recognize your friends and people in your family? Make up a special greeting with a friend or someone in your family. It can be a secret handshake, a gesture, a dance, or a word you say when you see each other.

# CLOTHESPIN PRONGHORN ANTELOPE

Pronghorn antelopes live only on the grasslands of North America. They eat grasses, bushes, and weeds that grow on the prairie. Think about people in your family. What parts of the world do your relatives come from? What foods does your family like to eat?

## WHAT YOU NEED:

- 3 wooden clothespins (not with a spring-clip)
- White craft glue
- Paintbrush
- White tempera paint
- Black marker

## WHAT YOU DO:

**1.** Glue two clothespins together.

**2.** Hold the third clothespin upside down, and glue it to the other two clothespins. The upside-down clothespin is the antelope's head. The other two clothespins are the antelope's body and legs.

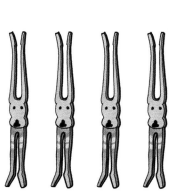

**3.** Paint two white stripes across the top clothespin, or across the two front legs of the antelope.

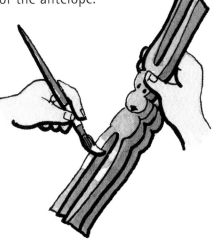

**4.** With the black marker, draw the antelope's eyes and nose.

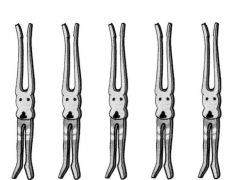

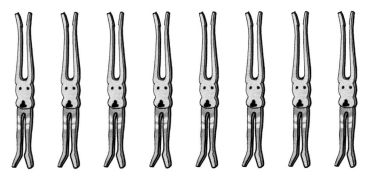

## FIELD NOTES

Pronghorn antelopes often live in big groups, called herds. In the summer, the herds are not very big. In the winter, the herds can have as many as 100 pronghorn antelope! Why do you think pronghorn antelope group together in a big herd in the winter? Imagine you are huddled together with friends or family. Would you feel warm or cold? How do you think the pronghorn antelope feel?

☛ **TRY THIS!** Make a few more clothespin pronghorns. See how many will fit on your paper prairie. Imagine you had a "herd" with 100 of them! Estimate how many paper prairies you would need to hold the clothespin antelopes.

## WHAT'S IN A NAME?

Pronghorn antelopes get their name from the "prong," or little piece, that sticks out on their horns. Pronghorns are one of the only animals that shed their horns each year. The outer covering, or sheath, of the horn falls off in the fall and grows back in the summer. How do you change each year?

# POM-POM MONARCH BUTTERFLY CATERPILLAR

Milkweed is one type of plant that grows on the prairie. The milkweed plant is also the only plant a monarch butterfly caterpillar will eat! The milkweed contains a poison that is not harmful to the caterpillar. To other animals, the poison tastes bad, and so the monarch caterpillar tastes bad. What things taste good and bad to you?

**WHAT YOU NEED:**

- Large white paper plate
- Green marker
- Small pom-poms (2 yellow, 2 black, 2 white)
- Scrap of black construction paper
- Child safety scissors
- White craft glue
- Wiggly eyes (optional)*

*Warning! Small beads pose a choking danger to young children. Grown-ups should control the supply and insert them into the project.

**WHAT YOU DO:**

**1.** Get a paper plate. Draw a large green leaf on the plate. This is a milkweed leaf.

**2.** Glue pom-poms onto the leaf in a curvy line, in this order: white, yellow black; white yellow black. This is the body of the caterpillar.

**3.** Cut out antennae from black paper, and glue them to the front and back of the caterpillar.

**4.** If you like, glue on wiggly eyes, too.

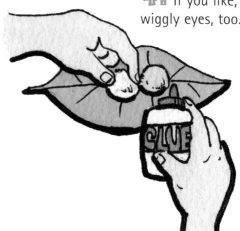

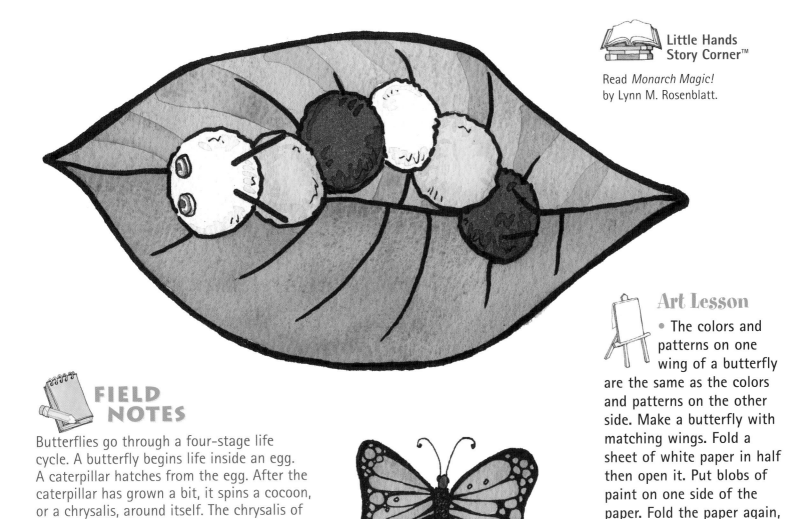

**Little Hands Story Corner**™

Read *Monarch Magic!* by Lynn M. Rosenblatt.

## FIELD NOTES

Butterflies go through a four-stage life cycle. A butterfly begins life inside an egg. A caterpillar hatches from the egg. After the caterpillar has grown a bit, it spins a cocoon, or a chrysalis, around itself. The chrysalis of the monarch butterfly usually hangs from a milkweed leaf. When the chrysalis hatches, the monarch butterfly comes out! Can you name four stages of human life? How about baby, child, teenager, adult? What stage are you in now?

## Art Lesson

• The colors and patterns on one wing of a butterfly are the same as the colors and patterns on the other side. Make a butterfly with matching wings. Fold a sheet of white paper in half then open it. Put blobs of paint on one side of the paper. Fold the paper again, and smooth the paper with your hand. Open the paper, and let the paint dry. Draw a butterfly's wings around the paint.

# PAPER-PLATE BISON

Long ago, bison were one of the most numerous animals of the prairie. People hunted the bison, and they almost disappeared. Today, most bison live on prairies in protected areas like national parks.

## WHAT YOU NEED:

- Pencil
- Large white paper plate
- Child safety scissors
- Black marker
- Brown crayon
- Glue
- Brown yarn (optional)

## WHAT YOU DO:

**1.** Draw the simple shape of the bison's head on a paper plate.

**2.** Cut away the sides of the paper plate so only the head remains. Save the rim you've cut off.

**3.** Draw bison features on the paper plate, including two large eyes. Color the paper plate brown.

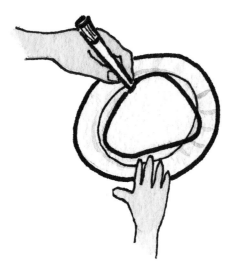

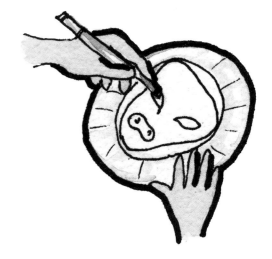

## WORDS TO KNOW

The American bison is often called a *buffalo*.

**4.** Cut out the eyeholes where you've drawn them.

**5.** From the cut-off part of the paper plate, cut out the bison's horns. Glue the horns to the top sides of the plate.

**6.** If you like, glue short lengths of brown yarn to the bison's chin.

**7.** Hold up the paper plate in front of your face for a bison mask.

☛ **TRY THIS!** Place two pairs of pants or T-shirts in the sun—one light-colored and one dark-colored. After about 10 minutes, feel each one. Which feels warmer? Which feels cooler? Darker colors absorb, or soak up, the sun's heat. So, in colder weather, darker fur is better because it keeps the bison warm.

## FIELD NOTES

In the winter, the bison's coat is dark brown, long, and shaggy. In the spring, the coat becomes shorter, and the color becomes a lighter brown. Why might a bison need longer, darker fur in colder weather? Why might shorter, lighter fur be better in warmer weather?

## LOOK AND LISTEN

Bisons grunt as they walk across the prairie. Hold up your paper-plate bison mask, and grunt when you walk!

# Welcome to the Wetlands!

A "wetland" is just what it says it is—a wet land. Wetlands are home to thousands of kinds of water and land plants, as well as animals, like water birds, fish, reptiles, and mammals. Long-legged water birds wade in the water among the plants, looking for fish and insects to eat. Alligators glide through the waters of the biggest wetland in North America—the Everglades of Florida.

What about wetland plants? First, imagine yourself sitting in a bathtub. Part of you is under the water, and part of you is above the water. This is similar to how some wetland plants grow. The upper part of the plant is above the water, and the bottom part is below the water. Some plants even grow underwater or float on top.

## What is special about wetlands?

Wetlands can be saltwater, freshwater, or both.

Wetlands can also be called swamps, marshes, or bogs.

A wetland may be as small as the shores of a pond, or as large as the Everglades. The plants and animals that live in each can be just as different. Let's discover some wetland plants and animals.

Look at the animals in this picture. Think about what makes the animal or plant perfect for living in the wetlands. How has the plant or animal adapted to its wetland habitat?

Which plant has leaves that are perfect for floating on top of the water?

Which plant grows below and above the water?

Which animal has legs that are perfect for wading into the water?

Which animal can swim in the water?

# EGG-CARTON WATER LILIES

The wetlands is the perfect place for water lilies to grow and bloom. The roots grab hold of the ground below the water, and the stem rises to the top of the water. At the top of the stem, a large leaf, called a lily pad, and sometimes a flower, rests on the water. Water lilies also grow in ponds and lakes.

## WHAT YOU NEED:

- Clean household sponge
- Child safety scissors
- Green paint in a dish or lid
- Blue construction paper
- Styrofoam egg carton
- Orange marker
- White craft glue

## WHAT YOU DO:

**1.** With a grown-up's help, cut the sponge into the shape of a water-lily leaf.

**2.** Dip the sponge in green paint, and press it to the blue paper. The blue paper is the wetland, and the print is the lily pad. Make several lily pads across the blue paper.

**3.** Cut apart the cups from a Styrofoam egg carton.

**4.** Cut the cups so they look like flowers. In the center of each, draw an orange burst.

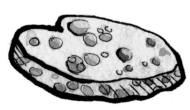

**5.** Glue the cups to the lily pads.

 **WETLAND SCIENCE**

Water lily leaves and flowers float on the water. Fill a large bowl or pot with water. Make a few Styrofoam flowers, and place them in the water. Do they float? Cut lily-pad shapes from the Styrofoam trays of fruits or vegetables. Place them in the water, too. Do they float? What will make them sink? Place small objects on the Styrofoam shapes to see how long you can keep them afloat.

*Adult supervision required when a child is near water.

 **FIELD NOTES**

Some water lilies bloom during the day, and some bloom at night. Each kind of lily opens at the same time each day and each night. Keep a log of the times you wake up go to sleep. Is the time the same or different each day?

☛ **TRY THIS!** The large leaves of water lilies are the perfect places for animals, like frogs, to rest. From large sheets of green poster board, cut out large lily pads. Place them around your room or outside. Hop from lily pad to lily pad.

 **Art Lesson**

• An artist named Claude Monet liked to paint water lilies. Use your egg-carton water lilies as a model. Set up a table with art paper and watercolors. (Cover the table with newspaper to protect the tabletop.) Make a painting of your egg-carton water lilies.

# PAPER-PLATE COTTONMOUTH SNAKE

Cottonmouths are snakes that swim in the water. They are very poisonous, and they will fight rather than slither away. If a cottonmouth has its mouth open, watch out! This is a warning to stay away.

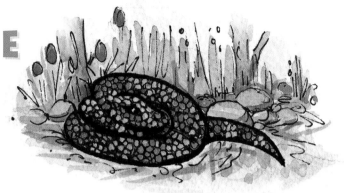

## WHAT YOU NEED:

- Large white paper plate
- Child safety scissors
- Brown crayon
- Dark marker

## WHAT YOU DO:

**1.** Cut off the rim of a paper plate in one long piece. This is the snake.

**2.** Cut one end of the rim into a triangle for the snake's head.

**3.** Color the snake brown. Draw on the snake's eyes and mouth.

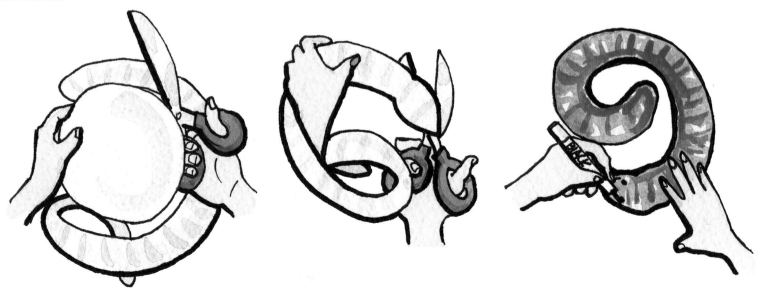

**4.** Cut a slit in the snake's tail. Curl the snake, and insert its body into the slit to hold the snake in place.

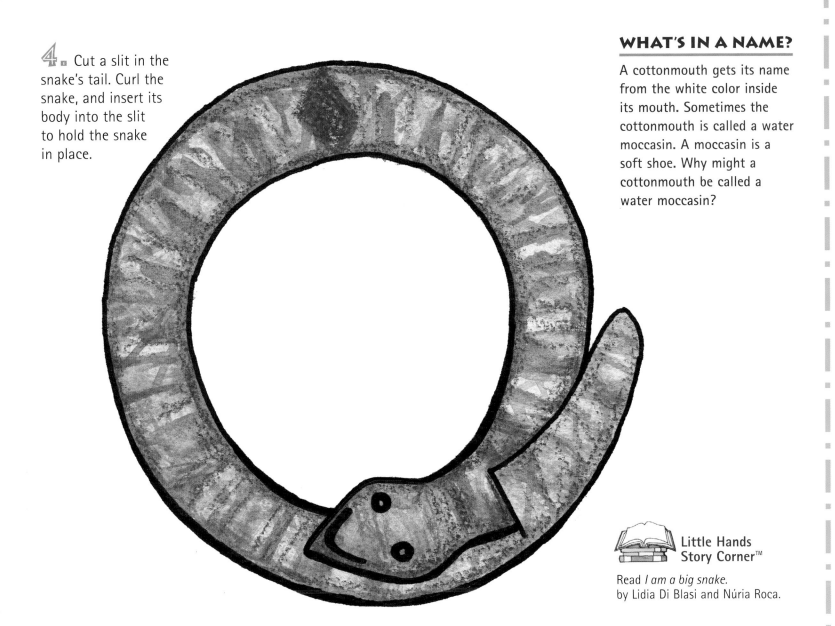

A cottonmouth gets its name from the white color inside its mouth. Sometimes the cottonmouth is called a water moccasin. A moccasin is a soft shoe. Why might a cottonmouth be called a water moccasin?

**Little Hands Story Corner™**

Read *I am a big snake.* by Lidia Di Blasi and Núria Roca.

# POPSICLE-STICK WHOOPING CRANE

Many birds that live in wetlands have long legs. These kinds of birds are called wading birds. The birds' long legs help them walk and stand, or wade, in the water. What other birds can you think of that have long legs? How about flamingoes?

## WHAT YOU NEED:

- Pencil
- 2 Styrofoam plates
- Child safety scissors
- White craft glue
- 2 Popsicle sticks
- Orange, black, blue, and green markers
- Regular scissors (ask a grown-up to help)

## WHAT YOU DO:

**1.** In the center of one Styrofoam plate, draw the outline of the whooping crane's body and head.

**2.** Cut away the rim of a Styrofoam plate. Cut out the body of the whooping crane from the center of the plate.

**3.** From the rim, cut out one whooping-crane wing. Glue the wing to the crane's body.

**4.** Draw the whooping crane's legs on each Popsicle stick. Glue the sticks to the back of the crane.

**5.** Draw features on the whooping crane's face with orange and black markers.

**6.** Turn the second Styrofoam plate upside down. Color it blue and green to be the wetland.

**7.** Cut two slits in the plate that match the position of the crane's legs.

**8.** Insert the Popsicle sticks into the slits to make your whooping crane wade through the wetlands.

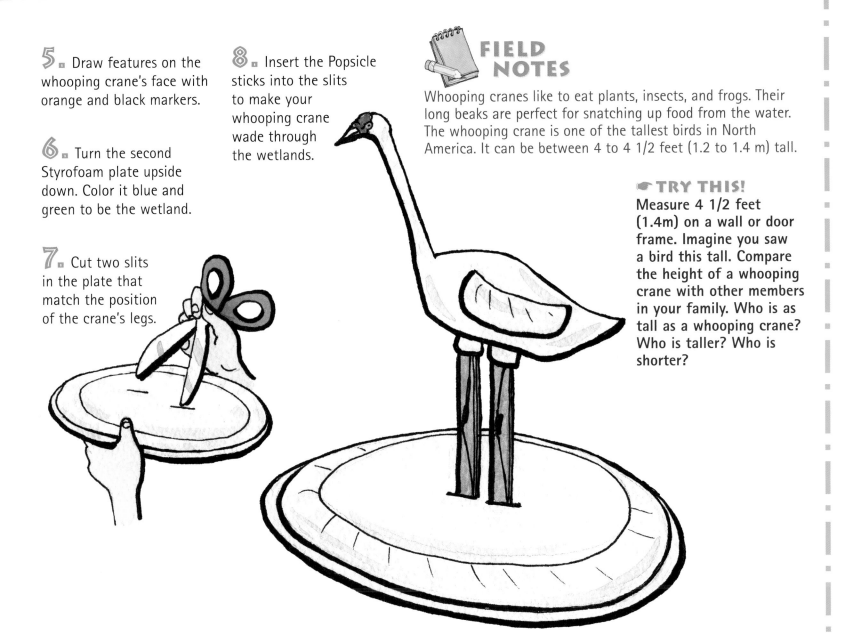

## FIELD NOTES

Whooping cranes like to eat plants, insects, and frogs. Their long beaks are perfect for snatching up food from the water. The whooping crane is one of the tallest birds in North America. It can be between 4 to 4 1/2 feet (1.2 to 1.4 m) tall.

☞ **TRY THIS!**
Measure 4 1/2 feet (1.4m) on a wall or door frame. Imagine you saw a bird this tall. Compare the height of a whooping crane with other members in your family. Who is as tall as a whooping crane? Who is taller? Who is shorter?

# PAPER-PUNCH DUCKWEED

Duckweed is a plant that floats on the surface of ponds, marshes, lakes, and quiet streams. It provides a tasty meal for fish and birds. How do you think duckweed got its name? If you said because ducks like to eat it too, you'd be correct!

**WHAT YOU NEED:**

- Small white paper plate
- Blue, green, and red crayons
- Hole punch
- Scrap of green construction paper
- Glue stick

**WHAT YOU DO:**

**1.** Color the center of the paper plate blue. Draw plants and flowers around the rim of the plate.

**2.** Using a hole punch, punch out holes from green construction paper. The punched-out circles are the duckweed.

**3.** Glue the punched-out circles to the blue center of the paper plate.

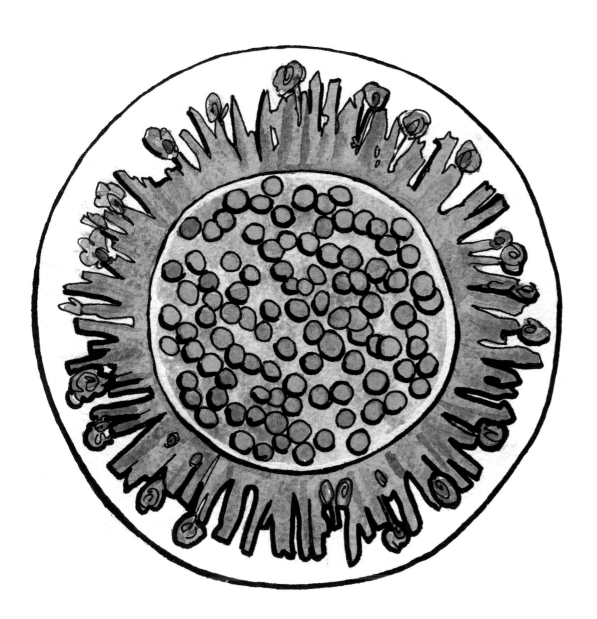

Duckweed is not only food for some animals, it is also protection. Some wetland animals, like frogs, snakes, and fish, hide within the duckweed to escape from predators—animals that want to eat them. Where do you sometimes hide when you play "Hide and Seek"? Do you hide under a piece of furniture or behind a tree?

### Art Lesson

• Look at the work of the French artist Georges-Pierre Seurat. Can you see the dots he used to create his paintings? This style of painting is called pointillism. Make your own pictures using this same technique. Punch out paper circles, and glue them down to make your picture.

# Welcome to the City!

When you hear the word *city*, you probably think of a place with lots of buildings, lots of people, and paved streets. Well, you're right! A city is a community made by people. Perhaps you live in a city, or you live near a city. Your town might be like a city because the buildings and streets were made by people.

Animals find places to live in a city, too. Although a city might not be a natural habitat—a habitat made by nature—many animals have found homes in city places made by people. For example, many cities have parks—open areas with green grass, trees, and flowers. Many birds, squirrels, and insects can live here. Plants and animals can live wherever they can find shelter and food.

## hat do most cities have in common?

Cities are places made by people.

Cities have tall buildings, paved streets, and green parks.

The biggest city in North America is Mexico City, Mexico. Over 22 million people live here. Big cities in the United States include New York City, Chicago, and Los Angeles. Big cities in Canada include Montreal, Toronto, and Vancouver. Let's meet some animals that have found ways to live in this human-made habitat.

A trip to the city can be overwhelming. In a forest, trees tower above you. In the city, buildings tower above you! Visit the city below and try to find the animals.

Which animal might march across the sidewalk?

Which animal can climb trees?

Which animal can perch on windowsills?

Which parts of this city block were made by people?

# CUT-PAPER CITYSCAPE

In a natural habitat, plants, like trees and cactus and flowers, grow. In a city, the buildings grow! People are always creating new and different buildings in a city. How do the buildings change where you live?

## WHAT YOU NEED:

- Pencil
- Ruler (optional)
- 1 sheet of black construction paper
- Child safety scissors
- 2 sheets of yellow construction paper
- Glue stick

## WHAT YOU DO:

**1.** With a pencil, draw the outline of buildings on the black construction paper. You might use a ruler to make straight lines.

**2.** Cut out the long row of black city buildings.

**3.** Line up the edges of the black city buildings against one sheet of yellow construction paper. Glue the black city buildings to the yellow paper.

**4.** From the second sheet of yellow construction paper, cut out small rectangles. Glue them to the buildings for windows.

## WHAT'S IN A NAME?

The tallest building in a city is called a skyscraper. Look at the picture below. Why is *skyscraper* a good name for very tall buildings?

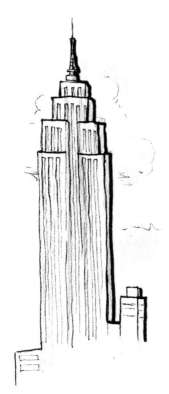

 **FIELD NOTES**

Cities are full of people. In fact, the places where the most people live are cities. In the United States, the most populated city is New York City. About 8 million people live here.

☞ **TRY THIS!** Draw a boy or a girl in one of the windows of your cityscape picture. Think about what you would tell this boy or girl about where you live. Then think about what the boy or girl might tell you about his or her life in the city. Tell your ideas to someone in your family.

 **Little Hands Story Corner™**

Read *Alphabet City* by Stephen T. Johnson.

# TREE-CLIMBING GRAY SQUIRREL

Gray squirrels are very adaptable animals. Before people built cities, gray squirrels lived in forests. People created parks and planted trees in the cities, and the squirrels now live here, too. Why might people want trees and parks in a city? What do you like about trees and parks?

## WHAT YOU NEED:

- White paper
- Pencil or dark marker
- Gray, brown, and green crayons
- Child safety scissors
- Popsicle stick
- Transparent tape
- Cardboard from a cereal box

## WHAT YOU DO:

**1.** Draw a squirrel on white paper. Color it gray, then cut it out.

**2.** Tape the squirrel to one end of a Popsicle stick.

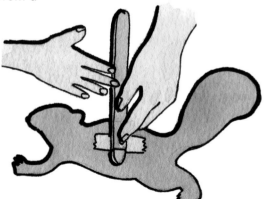

**3.** Cut off one big side from a box of cereal.

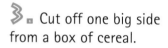

**4.** On the plain, gray side of the cardboard, draw a picture of a tree. Make the tree's trunk thick and tall. Color the tree's trunk and branches brown, and the tree's leaves green.

**5.** Cut a slit along one edge of the tree trunk. Ask a grown-up, if you need help.

**6.** Slip the Popsicle stick through the slit in front so the stick pokes out the back.

**7.** Move the squirrel up and down the tree trunk by moving the Popsicle stick behind the cardboard.

 **LOOK AND LISTEN**

Squirrels usually build their nests high up in the branches of trees. The fall is the best time to spot nests. Then the nests are more obvious, perched on the bare branches. Look for a squirrel's nest high up in a tree. It will look like a big, leafy pile, built between branches.

 **FIELD NOTES**

Gray squirrels like to eat seeds and nuts. In the fall, the squirrels begin to bury their food. Then in the winter, when seeds and nuts are hard to find, the squirrels have food already stored up. The squirrel can smell buried food under a foot of snow!

☞ **TRY THIS!** Play a game with a friend. Place a food with a strong odor in a cup. Tell your friend to close his or her eyes, and to sniff what is in the cup. Challenge your friend to guess the food. Some foods with strong odors are bananas, cheese, peanut butter, or cookies.

# GROCERY-BAG BROWN RAT

Squirrels and rats belong to the same large group of animals—rodents. Look at the picture of the rat on this page, then compare it with the picture of the squirrel on page 114. How are the animals the same? How is the rat different from the squirrel?

## WHAT YOU NEED:

- Brown grocery bag
- Ruler
- Pencil
- Child safety scissors
- Transparent tape
- Glue
- Wiggly eyes (optional)*

## WHAT YOU DO:

**1.** On the grocery bag, measure a square that is about 9" x 9" (22.5 cm x 22.5 cm). Cut it out.

**2.** Round off one corner of the square. That side of the square should look like the arc of a circle.

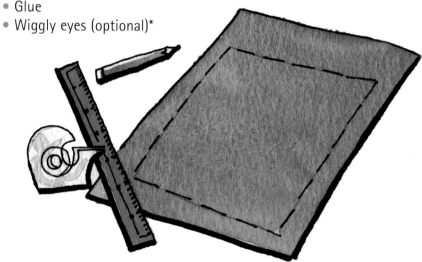

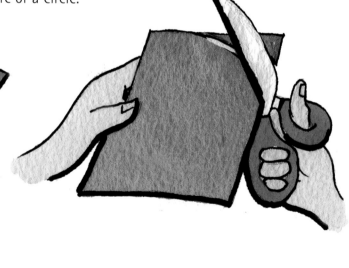

*Warning! Small beads pose a choking danger to young children. Grown-ups should control the supply and insert them into the project.

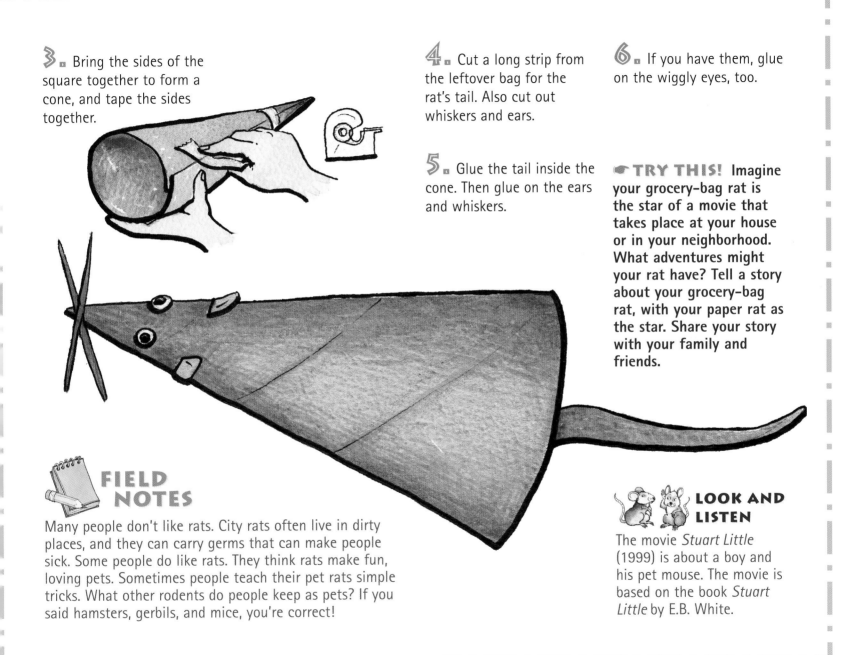

**3.** Bring the sides of the square together to form a cone, and tape the sides together.

**4.** Cut a long strip from the leftover bag for the rat's tail. Also cut out whiskers and ears.

**5.** Glue the tail inside the cone. Then glue on the ears and whiskers.

**6.** If you have them, glue on the wiggly eyes, too.

☞ **TRY THIS! Imagine your grocery-bag rat is the star of a movie that takes place at your house or in your neighborhood. What adventures might your rat have? Tell a story about your grocery-bag rat, with your paper rat as the star. Share your story with your family and friends.**

### FIELD NOTES

Many people don't like rats. City rats often live in dirty places, and they can carry germs that can make people sick. Some people do like rats. They think rats make fun, loving pets. Sometimes people teach their pet rats simple tricks. What other rodents do people keep as pets? If you said hamsters, gerbils, and mice, you're correct!

### LOOK AND LISTEN

The movie *Stuart Little* (1999) is about a boy and his pet mouse. The movie is based on the book *Stuart Little* by E.B. White.

# PAINT-DOT ANTS

Ants are insects. Like all insects, they have three body parts, six legs, and antennae on their heads. Ants look for food to bring back to their nests. In cities, ants might look for food on park tables, on picnic blankets, on sidewalks—even in apartments. A tiny crumb can bring out an army of ants! How do you think people can avoid an army of ants?

**WHAT YOU NEED:**

- Construction paper (any color except black)
- Black marker
- Child safety scissors
- Old magazine
- Glue stick
- Pencil with an eraser
- Black tempera paint, in a dish or lid
- Black ink pen

**WHAT YOU DO:**

**1.** On the construction paper, draw a simple pattern for a picnic blanket.

**2.** Cut fringes along the short sides of the construction paper.

**3.** Look through old magazines for pictures of foods. Try to find foods you'd like to eat on a picnic. Cut them out.

**4.** Glue the pictures to your construction-paper picnic blanket.

**5.** Here come the ants! Dip the eraser end of a pencil into a dish of black paint. Dab three dots, in a row, on the paper. This is the body of the ant. Remember—the ant's body has three parts.

**6.** Ants also have six legs and two antennae. Draw the ant's legs and antennae with a dark pen.

**7.** Repeat steps 5 and 6 several times to make several ants.

## FIELD NOTES

Ants are social insects. That means that ants don't live alone. Lots of ants live together in large groups, called colonies. The colony lives in rooms and tunnels that the ants dig underground. Each ant colony has a queen ant. She is the leader of the ant colony. The colony also has worker ants, who take care of the young ants, clean the underground rooms, and look for food. Colonies also have soldier ants, who guard the entrance of the ants' home. Each member of the colony has a job to do.

☞**TRY THIS!** Think about the jobs that the people in your family do that help your family. Write down their names, and list the things they do. Don't forget to include yourself! Then thank the people in your family for the jobs they do.

# STENCIL COCKROACH

Like ants, cockroaches are insects. They have lived on Earth for at least 250 million years. That means that cockroaches were around during the time of the dinosaurs. Compare the size of a cockroach with the size of a dinosaur. Isn't it amazing that the dinosaurs died out, and cockroaches are still with us?

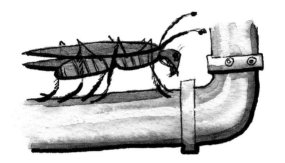

## WHAT YOU NEED:

- Pencil
- Paper plate
- Child safety scissors
- Construction paper (any light color)
- Clean household sponge
- Brown paint, in a dish or lid
- Thin paintbrush
- Yellow paint
- Brown and black markers

## WHAT YOU DO:

**1.** Draw an oval shape in the center of a paper plate.

**2.** Cut out the oval. Don't cut the rim of the plate. (Ask a grow-up to help you get started.) The rim of the plate is the stencil.

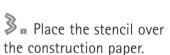

**3.** Place the stencil over the construction paper.

**4.** Dip a sponge into brown paint, and dab it over the stencil.

**5.** Lift the stencil. You've made a brown oval print on the paper! This is the body of the cockroach.

**6.** Move the stencil to another place on the paper, and repeat Step 4. Make as many brown ovals as you like. Allow the paint to dry.

**7.** To make the head, paint a yellow stripe on one end of each oval.

**8.** Use markers to draw the cockroach's legs, antennae, and eyes.

## Art Lesson

• Stencils are a fun way to make the same repeating pattern or picture. Try to make another stencil. Draw the outline of a shape, like a flower, on the center of a paper plate. Cut out the outline from the center. Place the stencil on a clean sheet of art paper. Dip a sponge into paint, and dab it over the stencil. Make a bouquet of stencil flowers!

## FIELD NOTES

Like rats, most people don't like cockroaches. Cockroaches can be pesky insects, creeping over kitchen counters and invading other places where people live. Scientists believe, though, that cockroaches play a very important role. Cockroaches that live in forests eat dead bugs and other tiny things. They keep the forest floor clean. If they live in a building, cockroaches are attracted to food that is left out in the open. How can people try to keep their homes free of cockroaches?

# SHOE-BOX-LID PIGEONS

Many cities have large numbers of pigeons. Pigeons look for food on the ground. City streets, sidewalks, park walkways, and other open areas often have food crumbs or even plant seeds. Pigeons walk along the ground, pecking for bits of food. If you wanted a group of pigeons to come to you, what could you do?

**WHAT YOU NEED:**

- Shoe-box lid
- Black marker
- White paper
- Crayons
- Child safety scissors
- Tape

**WHAT YOU DO:**

**1.** Angle the shoe-box lid so it looks tall, like a tall apartment building. On the inside of the shoe-box lid, draw rows of windows, like the windows on an apartment or other tall building.

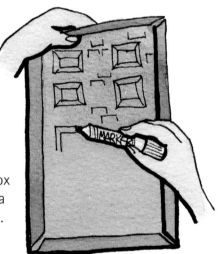

**2.** On white paper, draw one or two pigeons, like the one shown here.

**3.** Below the pigeon, draw a dotted line, then the outline of a short tab.

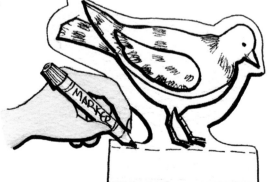

**4.** Cut out the pigeons, including the tab. Do not cut along the dotted line. This is a fold line.

**5.** Fold back the tab.

**6.** Tape the tab to the bottom rim of the shoe-box lid so it looks like your pigeons are standing on a city windowsill.

**Little Hands Story Corner™**

Read *Don't Let the Pigeon Drive the Bus!* by Mo Willems.

## FIELD NOTES

Like many birds, pigeons build nests with twigs. Because cities have more buildings than trees, pigeons often build their nests on building ledges, windowsills, or rooftops. The next time you visit a city, look up at the tall buildings. Try to spot a pigeon's nest.

## LOOK AND LISTEN

Male pigeons call, "coo roo-c'too-coo" when they want to attract females or defend their territory—the place where they live. When pigeons are startled or scared, they might make a call that sounds like: "oorhh!" Try to make these sounds, too.

# ANIMAL HABITAT INDEX

# ANIMAL HABITAT INDEX

# ANIMAL HABITAT INDEX

# More Good Books

## FROM WILLIAMSON

Welcome to Williamson Books! Our books are available from your bookseller or directly from Williamson Books at Ideals Publications. Please see the next page for ordering information or to visit our website. Thank you.

All books are suitable for children ages 3 through 7, and are 120 to 128 pages, 10 x 8, $12.95, unless otherwise noted.

## More Good Books by Judy Press

*Parent's Guide Classic Award*
*Real Life Award*
**The Little Hands ART BOOK**
Exploring Arts & Crafts with
2- to 6-Year-Olds

*Teachers' Choice Family Award*
*Parents' Choice Recommended*
**Sea Life Art & Activities**
Creative Experiences for
3- to 7-year-olds

ForeWord Magazine *Children's Book of the Year Finalist*
**All Around Town**
Exploring Your Community
Through Craft Fun

*Parents' Choice Recommended*
**At the Zoo!**
Explore the Animal World
with Craft Fun

*Parents' Choice Approved*
The Little Hands
**Big Fun Craft Book**
Creative Fun for 2- to 6-Year-Olds

**Around-The-World Art & Activities**
Visiting the 7 Continents through
Craft Fun

**Art Starts for Little Hands!**
Fun Discoveries for 3- to 7-Year-Olds

*Parent's Guide Children's Media Award*
**Alphabet Art**
With A to Z Animal Art & Fingerplays

*Early Childhood News Directors' Choice Award*
*Real Life Award*
**VROOM! VROOM!**
Making 'dozers, 'copters, trucks & more
*A Williamson Kids Can!® book for
ages 7 to 13*

*Parents' Choice Honor Award*
**The Kids' Natural History Book!**
Making Dinos, Fossils, Mammoths & More!
*A Williamson Kids Can!® book for
ages 7 to 13*

# More Good Books
## FROM WILLIAMSON

**Kindergarten Success**
Helping children excel right from the start
by Jill Frankel Hauser

*Parents' Choice Recommended*
**Easy Art Fun!**
Do-It-Yourself Crafts for Beginning Readers
(*A Little Hands® Read-&-Do book*)
by Jill Frankel Hauser

*Parents' Choice Gold Award*
**Fun with My 5 Senses**
Activities to Build Learning Readiness
by Sarah A. Williamson

*Parents' Choice Recommended*
**Early Learning Skill-Builders**
Colors, Shapes, Numbers & Letters
by Mary Tomczyk

*Parents' Choice Approved*
**Paper Plate Crafts**
Creative Art Fun for 3- to 7-year-olds
by Laura Check

*Parents' Choice Approved*
**Little Hands Create!**
Art & Activities for Kids Ages 3 to 6
by Mary Dall

*Parents' Choice Approved*
**Fingerplays & Action Songs**
Seasonal Activities & Creative Play for
2- to 6-Year-Olds
by Emily Stetson & Vicky Congdon

*Early Childhood News Directors' Choice Award*
*Parents' Choice Approved*
*American Institute of Physics Science
Writing Award*
**Science Play!**
Beginning Discoveries for 2- to 6-Year-Olds
by Jill Frankel Hauser

**Little Hands® Celebrate America!**
Learning about the U.S.. through
Crafts & Activities
by Jill Frankel Hauser

**Wow! I'm Reading!**
Fun Activities to Make Reading Happen
by Jill Frankel Hauser

*For dinosaur lovers of all ages!*
**In the Days of Dinos**
A Rhyming Romp through Dino History
by Howard Temperley
64 pages, 8 1/2 x 11, full color, $9.95